T0392276

THE
HOLY SPIRIT CALLING

A 40-Year Journey with the Holy Spirit

A. L. Istener

BALBOA.PRESS
A DIVISION OF HAY HOUSE

Scripture texts, prefaces, introductions, footnotes and cross references used in this work
marked NAB are taken from the New American Bible, revised edition © 2010, 1991, 1986,
1970 Confraternity of Christian Doctrine, Inc., Washington, DC All Rights Reserved.

Balboa Press books may be ordered through booksellers or by contacting:

Balboa Press
A Division of Hay House
1663 Liberty Drive
Bloomington, IN 47403
www.balboapress.com
844-682-1282

Because of the dynamic nature of the Internet, any web addresses or links contained in
this book may have changed since publication and may no longer be valid. The views
expressed in this work are solely those of the author and do not necessarily reflect the
views of the publisher, and the publisher hereby disclaims any responsibility for them.

The author of this book does not dispense medical advice or prescribe the use of any
technique as a form of treatment for physical, emotional, or medical problems without the
advice of a physician, either directly or indirectly. The intent of the author is only to offer
information of a general nature to help you in your quest for emotional and spiritual well-
being. In the event you use any of the information in this book for yourself, which is your
constitutional right, the author and the publisher assume no responsibility for your actions.

Any people depicted in stock imagery provided by Getty Images are models,
and such images are being used for illustrative purposes only.
Certain stock imagery © Getty Images.

Print information available on the last page.

ISBN: 978-1-9822-2812-5 (sc)
ISBN: 978-1-9822-2813-2 (e)

Balboa Press rev. date: 09/04/2020

Nihil obstat: Msgr. Chanel Jeanty, JCL
                        Vicar General and Chancellor
Imprimatur: Most Reverend Thomas G. Wenski
                        Archbishop of Miami
                        June 16, 2020

I DEDICATE THIS COLLECTION
TO YOU,
CHAMINADE-NATIVITY COMMUNITY OF FAITH

As a cradle Catholic I had been introduced to the Trinity - the Father, Son, and Holy Spirit early. As I grew I prayed to God the Father and Jesus, His Son, but the Holy Spirit meant little to me.

It was through you that I was introduced to the Holy Spirit Who changed my life. It was through you that my faith was reawakened and refreshed - It happened just as it did in Ezekiel's (dem) "dry bones" prophecy (37). The Holy Spirit came to dwell in me so that I could live!

Over the years, and particularly through these Words, the Lord, the community and I began a dialogue, and that led to a precious relationship.

It is my belief that these Words were sent to Chaminade-Nativity Community of Faith by the Holy Spirit for guidance and encouragement and to remind them of the depth of God's love for them.

To you, who are so very special to me - You brought me from a very dark place in my life into the light. You gave me hope. You gave me back my faith.

PREFACE

As you can see – I am a professional – a licensed clinical social worker (LCSW). Were I submitting a research paper to a journal, rather than having a book published, it would be necessary for me to state any bias I might have related to this subject. In that spirit I feel it necessary to inform the reader that although I do have a background in religious studies (a Master's degree from a Catholic University), training and experience as a Lay Minister, and am on the Pastoral Team of a prayer community, that the content of this collection is not intended to represent a direct, inspired communication with God, and in no way relates to the Scriptures or other writings by those authorized to speak for the church.

It does have the Imprimatur, however, which states that in the eyes of the Roman Catholic Church it is free of doctrinal or moral error.

This book is a layman's interpretation of the workings of the Holy Spirit and of the writings themselves. As for the author, and the question – Why me? Perhaps I will never understand it. Perhaps it is because I listened and wrote them down.

INTRODUCTION

If your purpose in reading this Introduction is to have a clear understanding of just what this book is – you may be disappointed and finish with more questions than answers. That has been my own experience in the preparation of it. For example: I could say "I do not consider myself the author of this book. I did not compose these writings. They were given to me by the Holy Spirit. I received them and wrote down them down."

Since I had already begun to receive my own personal response to my prayers, I knew these were not meant for me, but for my prayer community (and finally, to the larger community of believers). These Words differed in that they most often began with "My children", and they are written in pleural form.

Might I suggest that the subject of the sending and the receiving of communication with the deity can be so controversial that a simple format of question and answer may be the clearest way for me to share what I have found in my exploration of private revelation leaving further investigation up to you. It is you, ultimately who must interpret their meaning and make a judgment as to their authenticity. I have only received them for my community. I offer them to you.

Q: SO, WHAT'S IN THIS BOOK ANYWAY?
A: These are a collection of what I call "Words" - Words that I believe are from the Holy Spirit, written down just as they were received for my prayer group over a period of over 40 years. In searching for their meaning I discovered God Calling, a book written by two women looking for a reason to go on living. It was not only through prayer but by listening and writing down what they understood as God's response to their prayer that they were finally able to experience His presence in their lives.

Another "listener" was found in a missionary named Sarah Young who, after a lifetime of talking to God in prayer came to the realization that it had become a one-way monologue – with her doing all the talking. She decided to change that; instead, she would pray, then listen and write down what she thought was God's response. This moved her prayer life into a dialogue resulting in her book Jesus Calling.

[xi]

When I thought about it, I realized that I had been a "listener" too. I had already received responses to my personal prayer, often by journaling and soon a different kind of message was received, for my community. That is the subject of this book The Holy Spirit Calling. Like Sarah Young, I had listened too, and had written down the response that I believed to be that of the Holy Spirit. I wondered what the Lord had to teach our community. I listened and watched how most of us pray: we praise, express gratitude, intercession for others, and reflect. Perhaps we, too, like the other "listeners", did all the talking without expecting or waiting for a response. Did we also need to learn how to pray?

Q: IN ONE SENTENCE WHAT'S IT ABOUT?

A: Ours is a creative God who chose a unique way to remain with his church in order to guide it through its mission of evangelization by leaving us His Holy Spirit.

Q: WHO'S THE HOLY SPIRIT ANYWAY? BETTER YET - WHAT IS IT?

A: In the (Roman) Catholic faith the Holy Spirit is the third person of the Holy Trinity – Father, Son, and Holy Spirit, and is also known as Counselor, Spirit of Truth, Paraclete, Teacher, Comforter. Our belief is that when Jesus died on the cross He told us that he would not abandon us, his church, but would send us His Spirit who would remain with us to guide His church.

Q: WHY DO YOU THINK THESE "WORDS" WERE SENT?

A: To assure us of God's continuing presence among us.

Q: WHY WERE THEY SENT TO ME?

A: When I had finally entered them into my computer (almost 40 years down the road) I realized that they were meant to be kept (somehow) for my community, and possibly for others who needed encouragement and who needed to know that they are loved, just as they are, but when I found this Scripture, I knew:

> "So shall my word be that goes forth from my mouth; it shall not return to me Void, but shall do my will, achieving the end for which I sent it."

> (Is. 55:11)

Q: WHO SHOULD READ THESE?

A: Those who want to increase their awareness of God as he is present in their daily lives, in the circumstances in which they find themselves, and in others. Those who want to know how to communicate with God and develop a relationship with Him.

Q: YOU SAY YOU HAVE SOME OF THESE THAT ARE FOR YOU ALONE. HOW ARE THESE DIFFERENT?

A: Mine are specific to some of my concerns, goals.

I like writing things. I write poetry too, but mine doesn't sound like this.

These Words constantly say, "I love you", I don't.

These give advice, social workers don't give advice.

My Words are written in the singular, these in the pleural.

I edit everything I write. My edits are messy, with numbers and arrows all over the page.

Q: I'M HAVING A HARD TIME WITH THIS GOD AND SPIRIT THING

A: If all this sounds foreign to you we could say the author is anonymous. Or, if you have difficulty with the idea that I am trying to say that these Words were given to me by the Lord you could do as AA does and call my "Holy Spirit" my "Higher Power"- an entity outside of myself.

No matter where they came from, I did not write them. Nor did I make them up. I speak of its poetic writings as "my Words", and by that, I mean that I wrote them down over the years, did my best to find as many of them as I could, and copied them into the computer. The writing has not been edited or changed after being entered from the original scraps of paper into the computer.

It is my belief that the Words written on these pages were given to me by the Holy Spirit. I could not have written them myself. Although they are gathered and published in my name, I am not their author: their content is that of the Holy Spirit.

Q: OF WHAT BENEFIT IS THIS BOOK?

A: It is my hope that it helps readers to grow in an awareness that God is present here among us and that He continues to call us into relationship with Him.

Q: JUST INTERESTING TO KNOW

A: Notice that the Words have very little punctuation.

Often when you are getting near the end of a Word and you think you know where it is going, it has a special twist at the end.

Q: WHY ME?

A: I did not choose to publish this book. The Holy Spirit chose me. Perhaps it was a poor choice –it did take 40 years for me to even begin to realize why it may have been given to me.

WORD FROM 1974

My children, I love you so very much
Listen to my words
I speak to you of openness,
I ask that you open your hearts
Like the petals of a flower,
That I may rain my love upon you.
Let me feed you,
Let me nurture you
And let me protect you
For I love you
Jesus

WORDS FROM 1975

"I am like the river and the stream. Come, mingle with me, play with me and use me."

EMBRACING

"Don't embrace a vacuum (empty, nothing)
But reach out to each other
For in embracing each other
You embrace me."

Be like a tree that reaches its roots down into the earth
Seeking nourishment and sustenance.
I am the earth. I have abundance.
Take what you need to use. I will give it to you.
Sink down your roots deeply and widely – taking -
Your strong limbs will spread like open arms
To keep the weak sparrow's nest.
Your trunk will grow strong and hard from the winds that blow
And green, healthy leaves, in profusion will burst forth from your branches.
In the same way that your leaves take in carbon dioxide and give off oxygen, which
all things need to live.
I need you to come into contact with my people (you are my leaves),
So that as they come into contact with you
Their lives will change (because you have shown them Me).
You will be enabled to infuse them with new life, My life,
so that they are a new thing, because they met you.
By combining themselves with you, they are gaining Me and
becoming life (oxygen).

My people, I love you. You are like the crystal clear waters of my lakes. You are the well of my love for my people. Let them dip down into your cool waters and drink deep and full of me. Think of yourselves as obese with me, or as deep caverns filled with my love.

My people are in great need – they walk the hot roads of confusion and chaos. Allow them to dampen a cloth to cool their fevered brow. They walk in circles getting nowhere – reach out and break the chain. They grovel on their knees in the dry land when they can have Me – the everlasting water - continual refreshment, quiet, quenching their thirst.

I want to say "thank you" for being there for me to use. It is good for me to say "thank you" and to praise you, too, because all benefit by receiving praise and thanks, just as a child is best taught by his parent's praises.

I know that you love me so. Do not let the world's things dishearten you – I am with you and fill you with my lifetime spring. I touch you with a calm hand, a loving heart, and patient eyes that watch you in your flurry. I watch over you like a parent watches his child. As the child begins to walk – to investigate his world – to get into things, the parents are happy about his curiosity, courage and daring. They feel pride and joy in his new skills. I feel this same pride and joy. I will be there when you have pulled everything out investigated it, and tried to put things back together again. Just as your worldly parents are there, I am there to clean it all up when you finish.

I want you to live your lives like a bright, fun loving puppy. I am your master, you are my playful pups. You love me and want to be near me. You lie at my side sometimes, restfully, or take a quiet walk with me as I think. But it is joyful to have you wake me up sometimes in the morning, nipping my hand over the side of the bed, or putting your head in my hand for me to scratch it. You want me to hurry up and wake up – to greet the day, and especially to be with you. It makes me happy to wake up that way.

I like to just lie there, at first and watch your springy step, and wiry wagging tail shaking faster in anticipation of each movement I will make – your eyes urging me to "get up and play with me", ears cocked forward, waiting for my hand to move so that you can pounce upon it.

And so begins your day...in anticipation.

I want you to be healthy, springy, playful, hopeful – to greet your days watching for things to happen to you. I glory in this because it shows me to be a master who:

> Cares for the ones he loves
> Plays with them
> Feeds them well so that they are strong and able to do this

You, my puppy, can be like this because you trust me.

"My children,
How I love you!
Become as little children"

(This is my understanding of what the Lord was trying to say to me)

An infant is taken care of (God takes care of us).
(ie. Lk 12:7 "...even the hairs on your head are counted! ....")
The infant does not immediately "love" (its caretakers) –
But accepts care (feeding, changing, burping),
And from that learns to trust and to love.
It learns to trust that when it is in need, things are provided for it.
The baby starts cooing – (responding to "mother") – "giving back".
Age 2: Baby learns to give and receive reciprocally (to give back).
You give to me – I give back to you
A relationship is established, both giving what the other needs
This is called love.

God tells us that he loves us,
Which is different than "I care for you".
"I love you" is a more refined relationship.
It means that we already know and have accepted his "care for us" and are responding to it.
People who find it difficult to trust have not had anyone to take care of them or have not been able to allow anyone to do so.

Don't look down your nose at anyone.

Don't be smug because you know I love you.

Don't think I love only you.

Yes, even the ones you find disgusting.

I love them as much as I love you.

Don't assume that they don't know me or love me.

Only I know what is truly in their hearts.

Don't be cruel to a heart that's true.

Forgive them as I have forgiven you.

Love them as I love you.

Then they will see Me in you.

Loath the sin and not the sinner.

WORDS FROM 1976

I call you forth into my suffering, into my love.
With all the thorns and thistles, bursts forth the triumph
I do not call you to anything else –
To death to yourself, life to me,

It is a long road to the final crown
It is a long road to the final peace, until you rest in me
Your calls are all the same, to die to yourselves
That I may live in you

Do not say "not now", "later",
That is how the others do
But bend and pick up your cross
And be on your way to loving me

Love is not difficult
It is giving all
Letting me be all to you
Leaning on me – letting me love you

WORD FROM 1978

Come to me as little children - ask advice,

Like children come to their father to talk things over.

I have been getting you ready for a mighty work

I have nurtured you - filled you -

Go out and do for others. Are you ready?

I have much work for you,

But you must do it with compassion, tenderness.

There is great power in your praises.

My presence must be made known to my children through you.

I need you to be my hosts of love

You are to be love

My word will not come back empty.

It is through you I will do my work.

Give yourself to me completely.

I want a people of uncommon love.

Let me use you.

(Received at a day of Renewal)

WORDS FROM 1979

Love me, love my people
Reach out and cling to each other for dear life
For it <u>is</u> your life.

I want you to need each other
As you need me.
It is humbling to tell another that you need them,
Are not sufficient without them.

This is especially true in close
Marital relationships and family relationships
But we grow, also
In each other's uniqueness

About 1979

I have called you, my children, to holiness. This call implies suffering. You are called to assume the sins of the world, as did my Son. By his example you are expected to die to yourselves, take on the pain, sin and suffering of your fellow man and offer it to me.

I have called you out from the others. I will shower you with my grace to sustain you, as I did my Son. You may groan and whine under the impact, but I hear you and share the load with you.

Those of you who have been called forward, closer than the others, must be more set apart from man – more detached from the world. I call you in a special way and increase my graces accordingly. With greater intensity comes greater struggle. Because I have loved you so much, great will be your suffering. There is much sin in the world. You live in troubled times. I feel a great compassion for my people. I pour out my compassion, but some are so far from me they cannot experience my forgiveness. This is the work of those who have openly responded to my call for a closer union – to bring in my sheep. Help them to accept my love. Have compassion for all living things – especially those farthest from me, for those are the hardest for me to reach. You, however, can reach them, if you but respond to my call of love. I beckon to you, my people, let me love you.

WORD FROM 1980

ABOUT 1980

I glory in you,
For you are a just and holy people
I have voice in the world through you
Through you I bring justice to the world
Yes, you are truly
Justified and made holy -
Bring my people to me

WORDS FROM 1981

You are, indeed, a worthy and holy people. I am well pleased.
You do me honor with your praise!

I want to gift you further with the fullness of my presence.
It pleases me to be with you.
Are you aware that this is why I left myself with you
In the Eucharist and the Holy Spirit?

Each time my Son is sacrificed in the Eucharist,
I give myself more fully to you.
Each time He is resurrected in you when you have received it
I am again fulfilled in you.

My Spirit dwells within you.
My church, my eternal flame.
I dwell within each of you,
Yet within the whole (church)

I am with you always.
Until the end of time.

My people –
Do not try to be profound
My message is a simple one
Come to me humbly,
With contrite hearts –

Yes, I do want to radically change you,
But gently, with love
Compassion and simplicity.

It is so easy.
A simple formula
Come to me and open yourselves up
To all I have to offer
And I will do the rest.
(At a conference)

I love you my people
I continue to tell you how precious you are to me

I need you to minister to my people
They are in such distress! Their pain is profound!

I'm sure you understand; you have felt such pain.
Reach down, deep within your heart and help others.

I have given you this command:
If you are my followers I ask you to live in service to your fellow man

My people:

Be kind to yourselves

The road to salvation is long and hard

Prepare yourselves with some reserves

I do not condemn you

Why do you condemn yourselves?

I am pleased with you and how you are living your lives

Relax, live in me

I live in you

You're already there – enjoy

Especially parents with families

By living your commitments you are fulfilling my word

Just be

Take care to minister to each other's needs for individual prayer

You are with me now

You are each called, no less than David

You are each chosen

You have each, also, been called by name

WORDS FROM 1982

I have placed my seal upon you
I have marked you for my own.
Given this security,
Purify yourselves
That you might be made worthy.
Sacrifice
And do works of mercy
Grow in relationship with me
Learn to love one another
Be my presence to those with whom you work
Live the life of my Son.
Then I shall surely raise you up
And make you whole again
You will experience my love in a new way
Forgetful of yourself
In union with me.

This scripture (Rom 2:4) is your inheritance,
This scripture is your heritage
Be "nourished" in this word
It is a book about relationships
My relationship with you,
Your relationship with me,
Our relationship with others in the world
It is the answer
It will leave an everlasting flavor in your lives.

I want you to ask for all your needs
None are too small
Of course my greatest desire
Is that you accept my
Invitation to a closer walk with me

Who is it you glorify in your life?
What is it you choose?
Be sure that it is of ultimate value
For what you choose, you live
And upon this you will be judged

Do not take lightly what I have told you tonight.
My precepts are set down.
You have them
You will be held responsible
For the knowledge you have been given.
You are no longer ignorant of the truth
You have it,
Ingest it
Make it your own
Know me through my word.
Know me in my word.
Know me with my word.
I gave it to you because I love you
So that you might know the way

My son was the fulfillment

So you, too, are the fulfillment

As he was the hope of the (others)

As he lived in my love

You too live on in my love.

WORDS FROM 1984

As you walk toward me –
No – you are not yet perfected
However, I see no blemish
To me – you are near to perfect
I accept you just as you are
With all your imperfections

Observe the variety of wildlife in the jungle...
See the multitude of designs
Within each species of tree and vine.
Look at the configurations of clouds...
See how they intermingle
With the rainbow of colors
In the sunrise and sunset.
There are the multitude of earthy things
That burrow below the ground
And fowl that watch the sky.
In My natural law I have set down my pattern.
There is value and truth
In following this secure way,
The way I have set before you –
In the order of my universe.
But because you are man,
You must not necessarily be limited
By the structure of the rest of nature,
For these are in submission to you.
You are called, also, to something more
You are called to that creative exchange
Which surpasses all else.
For you are called out into transcendent love –
Limitless, boundless, self-giving.
You are called out of yourselves,
To pour yourselves out generously for each other.
Do not turn away.
I beckon to you...
As you turn to your brother,
You turn to me...

As you emerge into the new wave
Do not forget from whence you came
You came from within a tradition
Just as you change from within to without
You move on to the future from the past

You are a people of the new wave
But you come from within the old
Just as you cannot separate
The crest of the wave
From its return

I am within and without
Above and below
Among, but set apart
I walk before you
Yet at your side

Never forget that I am with you
I am part of you –
As you are part of me
I dwell within.

How could two who abide in mutual love
Live differently?
It is not only that you love me
Recall – It was I who loved you first!

You are so precious to me
I am yours
(Your most precious gift
Who dwells within)
As you are mine.

I sent my Word to all the world

It was you who received Him

I accept your praise and thanksgiving graciously

You are truly a glorious and blessed people
Do not think, however,
That is you who make yourselves holy.
It is in, through, and with me
That you are perfected and made holy
It is in the name of my Son, Jesus and the Holy Spirit
That you are transformed.

I am the beginning and the end
I am the content
I come down and walk with you
In your joys and your suffering
And it is being there with you that
I raise you up
Just as my Son came down,
Suffered, as you do,
Died and was raised.
It is through, with, and in Him that
You are able to enter into your suffering,
As He did, and be lifted up,
Again, as He was.
So never forget that I came down and
Am with you, as I was with Him,
And I will raise you up, as I did Him,
If you will let me, as He did.

Begin your journey toward me
Do not let worldly affairs deter you
Throw yourselves in my arms
For there, and only there
Will you find comfort and the strength to go on
Never forget you are my chosen people
Many before you have wished for what you have
Many after you will wish for it too
What a prize you have in your faith
Offer Jesus to the Father
Offer yourself
Your life to the Father
Your sacrifice is made perfect
The world is consecrated to God by you

WORDS FROM 1985

Never forget that you may be the only avenue of salvation
>For your fellow man

It may be that through you is the only way that he
>May allow me to touch him

Stay open to my promptings
>And go where I direct you

If you will empty yourself
    Of the idols of your day
Your worldly cares and preoccupations

I will enter there
    Within the emptiness
And fill you with my Holy Spirit

Opening the door to your heart is only the first step

The ensuing walk is often hard

The road is rocky and full of dust

It entails giving up your life –

Dying to self –

Washing off that dust from your brother's feet,

Even when your own are covered

The walk is hard

And often lonely.

Rest assured, however,

That I walk along with you,

At your side, as on the road to Emmaus

I continue to call you out

As I called you from Egypt

But do not grumble as they did in their wanderings in the dessert

Take up your cross

It is necessary for you to accept it with quiet humility

You are not to be like the others
Fighting, bickering, flailing out at each other
Especially within your families
I send the spirit of peace, order and contentment –
Yes, even joy and hilarity.
But this is not easy for me to accomplish
For the world teaches retaliation, anger, hatred of one another
It teaches us to hit and hurt where others are most vulnerable
To irritate, aggress
This is not that to which you were called
Turn back to me and observe my goodness
Patience, peace, generosity of spirit, kindness
Do this – become this – live in love and you will be my disciple.

I do not call you into poverty
But into a richness of Spirit
I call you into the Holy of Holies
Where only you and I are present
Come before me today
Do not wait until the end times –
Now is the time for us to talk together
In this way we can work out your salvation together
You will not be alone.
And you will have the benefit of my guidance
In your life here and now!
Indeed, you will be rich in Spirit.

Again – My people -
I have loved you first
But I do enjoy your
Praise, thanksgiving and love
Is it not glorious to live in reciprocal love?
This is not, however a 50- 50 love
I pour myself out to you

Relax – be yourself.
Remember,
It was I who created you.
Of course I accept you
Just as you are.
Look around you and see
The rest of the beauty
I have created.
Would you criticize a flow'r?
Do you find fault with
The perfection of a baby?
What of the complexity
Of the solar system?
Of how much more value
Are you than these things?
I have made the intricacies
Of your eyes.
I have developed a complex circulatory
System within you.
I re-create many cells throughout
Your whole body every day.
Why, then, would I not see
My most perfect creation
As totally acceptable to me?
You are my most perfect work –
You are my work of art.
You are part of me.
You are me,
As I have placed myself within you.

If you will but open yourselves to me

I will inspire you –

Enlighten your minds and spur you on to my work

I am your inspiration.

I am the wisdom, knowledge, understanding

I give you these gifts to draw others to me

If you will but open your mind

I will penetrate your heart and make you a fitting instrument

WORDS FROM 1986

I AM a God of infinite variety

I AM the God who designs each cloud formation

I AM the God who imprints your individuality upon the end of your finger

Who would imagine, therefore,

That my work within you would be repetitious? Would be as that of another?

Similarly, I call you each personally, individually.

I call you each in a different way.

Look, my People, look and discern -

Look deep within yourselves and without-

Among those who love you

See my direction for you alone

And follow it – with courage

I call you to an openness to receive me
I call you to be open to my Word

Had I not told them
That on the 3rd day I would rise again?
Yet they did not expect me -
They had forgotten
They had not understood
I have gifted you all, subsequently with understanding
Open yourselves to recognize me
For still I am often there when you do not expect me
Be open

I challenge you to walk the walk
I will direct you along the way
Observe the potholes – the weaknesses in the road
You may want to straddle them or avoid them,
But ultimately, if you want to be made whole,
I will fill them with new material
It is through them that others, too,
May make fuller use of the road
To reach their destination.

8/18/86

As I come to point the way to my Father
And Mary always points the way to Me
So are you to point the way to my Father
For he is the culmination of all that is good
Of all that is pure
Of all that is sacred
And all life points to Him
Glory to God our Father!

WORDS FROM 1987

CLIMB THE HIGHEST MOUNTAINS

Do not walk upon the plains
For those who walk the plains
Have not known me as you have.

Have compassion on them
They have not known
The inspiration of my Word.
They have not felt me within their very being
They have not experienced me
Walking with them in their daily lives.

You know me
You know my voice
You feel my presence
I am within you
I am among you
I am part of you

Go among the world
As if you know this
Go as if my presence
Has made a difference in your life.

Do not gorge yourselves with life's riches

Do not attach yourselves to the world's goods

Empty yourselves

And from that emptiness

My gifts ill flow

My abundance enriching all

Be like the flame on a candle
Dance around the wick (God)
Shed warmth and comfort
Enkindle the lives of others
While joining with Him
In shedding the light

The way to the Father
    is not disordered
    and fragmented
The way is that of
    discipline
    and order
Lead lives which exemplify
    these virtues

I am not a scattered, fragmented God!

I gather all things together into a whole.

I am that God who works all things together for good

Do not work for causes which separate

Support those things that unify

Live in harmony with each other

Be open and sensitive

For it is through this openness and flexibility

That you become one of the others – and not separate

Remember, you are only part of the whole.

Dear Children,

I beseech you to take up the way of holiness today

I love you and I want you to be holy

I do not want Satan to block you on the way.

Dear children,

Pray and accept all that God is offering you

On a way which is bitter.

But at the same time,

God will reveal every sweetness

To whoever begins to go on that way,

And he will gladly answer every call of God.

Do not attribute importance to petty things,

Long for heaven.

Thank you for your response to my call.

My people
I want you to maximize your potential -
To be what you were meant to be
I have called you out of yourselves
What exceeds yourself is Me!
Step out and take the risk
For it is your completeness,
Your wholeness,
Your living in fullness
That I am best made manifest

Do not focus on pettiness
I am a grand God
A God of Majesty
Yet I am a gentle God.

Do not get stuck on the little things
I will push them aside
And they will become inconsequential
Focus on the important
My relationship with you!

WORDS FROM 1988

To all things there is a season

A dichotomy

A pushing and a pulling

A giving and a taking

When you have given all

And feel depleted

That is when I give, through you

Grasp those moments

When you can receive, and be filled

Pay attention to those moments

Don't let them pass you by-

We need each infilling

For often, humanly speaking

We are empty

Be in unity

For though I am a diverse Spirit,
I am of one heart and mind.

Fragmentation reaps chaos
Disunity, separation
Randomness is meaningless

Union is reasonableness
Through it we are able
To Discern and understand

Come together in peace
Be with me
In union with me.
(At Mass)

My voice is one of conviction –
Not of doubt or confusion
Where I am there is clarity of thought.
You will know – You will know
Without a doubt
For your prompting will be
Direct, clean, without distraction
For I will not let you alone
And what would you do if I did?
You would want me to pester you again.
Do you not enjoy it
When your children brush your lives?
Do you not want them around?
It is so with me –
I revel in being in your lives –
Interacting with you –
Working it out
Arguing with you
Tell me your side
I'll tell you mine.
Let's work this out together
It does not always have to be 100% my way
So let us work together
What you lack, I will supply
What you are not, I am
What a team we can be together

SALVATION IN MY BROTHER

Root out the evil in your lives
Do not let the sun set
Before you examine yourselves
For any evil you may have done
Acknowledge it, bring it before me
Reconcile yourselves next with your brother
For I do not observe you in isolation
But in relation to your brother.

It is through him, also, that you will be perfected
Remember that –
Your salvation rests among you
Purify yourselves through your brother.

Do not run, scattered, helter-skelter-
Wait for my direction
Await my prompting
Be ready
But do not move until I tell you to
You will know for I will open the door wide
I will prepare the way.

Remember it is not your way it is mine
And I know the best way to get there
I can see the whole picture
Your gift is limited

Would I lead you along the wrong pathway?
Would I plan less than the best for you?
Do not become confused
Between the plans of man and mine.

You will recognize mine –
They are clear and without deceit (political)
I will place my people in positions
Where they can be of most use to me and my people.
Don't waste your efforts on man's deeds –

Await my guidance –
I will send those to you to show you the way –
Await – discern, and obey
And together we will touch the hearts of man.

Be quiet achievers
Be encouragers
Be affirmers
Be "yes" people

No negativity
No balking

YOU ARE IMBUED WITH THE SPIRIT OF FREEDOM

For you are entrusted with the Spirit of Freedom

1. You are gifted with the Spirit of Freedom
2. You are formed with the Spirit of Freedom
3. You are molded with the Spirit of Freedom
4. You are enfolded in the Spirit of Freedom
5. You are worthy of the Spirit of Freedom

You are indeed a holy people
You are blessed indeed
For I have blessed you
I have set my seal upon you
I have filled you with myself.

Do not think you are as others
For you have been set apart
But I have placed upon you, too,
A responsibility
A way of living that is mine.

You cannot afford to be as others
For I am within you
And you are different because of this
I am present to others
Often just because of you

Because of you some area of darkness will be lit
Some misunderstanding resolved
Some pain relieved
I go into the world because of you
One who has given up will hope again.

Yes, it is through you that I become manifest
It is by you that I enter into the lives
Of your fellow men and women
It is in you that I dispense my grace
I send my Spirit –
You are my Presence.

WORDS FROM 1989

Do not lock yourselves into a preconceived idea of Me,

For I am manifest in a variety of ways,

For I am multi-variant multi-colored,

Such as a kaleidoscope

And my sign, the rainbow......

BE MY INSTRUMENTS

If you pray for wisdom
I want you to recognize it when it comes.

You all have your own unique character and qualities,
As do the musical instruments.

You will be gifted according to my plan
In accord with your own individuality.

To one may be given a booming loud noise,
To another a sweet refrain,

To some a clear cut, straight forward sound
For each is called and gifted for my mission.

You will receive the wisdom that will be pleasing
To the ears of those who hear my song.

And who are you to say you are not worthy?

Did I not create you?

Make you above all things, in my image?

If others were to think they were not worthy

Who would I use?

I would have no hands or feet,

No voice, no ability to touch the lives of others

Through friend, relative, husband, wife, daughter, son.

Be there for me to use,

Overcoming any sense of insecurity or unworthiness

For you are mine and mine alone.

I bless you; I shower you in blessings and my giftedness.

Break out and be all that you can be in my name.

I empower you!

You are my precious ones.

Accept my love

You are worthy!

CONQUOR YOURSELF

But my people,
Do not wait until you are drowning.
Come to me with your smallest...(concerns)...
In that way I will come to reside in you
And make my home in you.

Thrust your anchor
Deep into my rock
And you will never
Venture far from me.
Then go out in faith and trust
Do not be a stone face
But reflect my joy,
Your knowledge that indeed
You have been called.
Trust in me
That I will not allow you to fall
Peace is to follow you.

The fruit of your pain
May serve as a burnt offering

But, as I have said,
This is not sufficient

You must pour yourselves out
Empty yourselves

Minister to your brothers and sisters
And to the world
So that I can be made manifest.

WORD FROM 1990

Do not concern yourselves with the attacks of the world
Do not allow them to penetrate your interior.
They may prick you from without
Or slam against your exterior,
But within we are impenetrable together.
There is a place within
Where we are joined together as one.
Remember I am within you
This is a special place
For you and I to be together
Where none can intrude
Together we are strong and at peace.
It is from this font
That flows the fruit of creativity
That aids you in ministering to my people.
Recognize that you have this special place.
Enter there often and let me minister to you –
Bind your wounds inflicted by the world.
Come be with me
I always await you.

"I am the glorified Christ
It is in and through me
That your salvation is accomplished.
Do not forget that it is in and through me
That you are perfected."

THE GRAPES

I have gathered the harvest
I do not discard those blemished
But cast them with the whole
To blend a most perfect wine
Through which I will nourish the world.

THE TREES

Be as the multicolored, variegated as trees in the rain forests
For it is through you that I breathe life to the world.
Rooted in me, stand stalwart against the evil.
Multivariate, yet unified, blended together.

WORDS FROM 1991

ALL ROADS LEAD TO ME

Never lose trust in me
Always know that I am there
Perhaps in the shadows
Or along the side of the road
Perhaps not right alongside you
But I am with you.

The path may perhaps not be smooth
But filled with pebbles or even boulders
Yet all roads lead to me.

Tale care in how you walk the path.
Use kindness, gentleness, peace and love
For you know not with whom you walk
Recall the road to Amadeus.

WORDS FROM 1992

LIVING WATERS

Let not your waters be still
These are living waters
Allow my Spirit to stir them up
They are to be effervescent
So that my life may pour forth through them
To quench the thirst of the seekers.

MY SPIIRIT IS ALIVE

Awaken!

Do not doze!

My Spirit is alive in you

It is there!

It is within!

Crying to come out -

WORDS FROM 1993

It is I who dwell in your praises
It is I who dwell in your love.
Do not complain
Or behave in an irascible manner
For you know not to whom you speak
Dwell in praise
Dwell in love.

In all circumstances glorify me
In all circumstances glorify me
In all circumstances exalt me
In all circumstances exalt me
In all circumstances extol me
In all circumstances extol me
Although many circumstances
In which you find yourselves
Are not of my making –
They are your own choices.
I will be with you within the circumstance,
Within the situation
For I am with you in all things.

Be stalwart
Be alert
Be ready
For I have things for you to do

Perhaps they may not be as you expect
So be alive
Listen!
I will speak to you!

I will send you on your way
If you will only be alert to my direction!
Be mindful of me at all times of the day!
Be ready to go out

Take heed my people!
Hearken to my word!
For the time may come
When I am not so close to you –
When you may not hear my voice.

At that time you will flounder around
Be unsure of my direction
Wonder of my presence
For you may not experience it
It does not mean I am not there
Only that you are not able to
Perceive me at that particular time.

Drink your fill
When the water is high
When the well is full
For you know not the future –
Of what is to come.

As this bread and wine
Is changed into my body and blood
I want you, too, changed
Do not leave here tonight
Unchanged

You are indeed a servant people

You are my hands and feet

You are my body

I depend on you to touch each other

To actually be with each other

To listen to each other

To be my presence amid the chaos

Others do not always hearken to me

Do not seek me

Look to me for direction to carry out my plan in their lives

But to you who do

Glorify my name!

Be there for me

As I am often there for you

Even when you do not seek me

I am there because you are loveable, and I love you

Love your neighbor and enemy for me

Because you are there

You are my presence

And you must be loving

I urge you, go on, go forward – I will part the waters.

Though you come up against seemingly insurmountable odds,

As did the Israelites in crossing the Red Sea -

I walk before you

I walk with you

I walk among you

I walk behind you

I walk along side you

I am your brother, your father, mother, sister,

Yes even may be your enemy.

Do not let trifles detour you

Do not be overly cautious

Do not hesitate

Move on

The time is now

Not tomorrow, or next week, or next month

It is now

You need to be ready now.

Right now!

When you bring from dark to light
That which is right
And it is observed with clarity
Discerned to be true
Done with pure motive
And a wish to serve,
It is dispensed with love
And brings life

Turn away from evil
　　And toward that which gives life

I give voice through the least of these
Through the poor, the disenfranchised
For through them salvation is sent.

I enter those dark places within you
Even, sometimes those to which I am not invited
I root out the poisons
Pry loose the kernel, the seed of evil, sin
That you might be washed clean and purified

THE FLOWER

I sprinkle you with dew
Soak your leaves with the rain
...(Let me?)... shine on you
Come forth, like a blossom,
I coax you forth
Bloom, and put forth seed

Open yourselves as the flowers and grasses receive the dew
As the waters run home to the sea,
Allow my presence to saturate your being
And flow forth to the larger body

THE GUARDIAN OF YOUR SOUL

Filled with brilliant fuchsia, red and gold,
Heavy laden with vine.
Full bursts of color, and green with lacy leaf,
Bulbs, buds, flowers in full bloom,
Ferns, the leaves with thorns, betwixt, between,
And full blanketed with green.
This is, indeed, my view, when I peer deep down
And look within your soul

You are a most blessed and holy people
And it is through you
Through your most inner self
That I renew the church

WORDS FROM 1994

you are not as stagnant lakes
you are crystal clear running streams
you are in constant creation
always in process
always unfolding and becoming.

like a rose
open up
unfold
be willing to
expose your heart

(Written the day after Valentine's Day)

Cherish each other,
Minister to each other,
Value each other.

Do not let any among you wander away,
Follow them and bring them back.

I like my people
to be disciplined.

In that way
you are prepared to confront the evil
in your lives
and obstacles in your paths.

5/3/94

You are my most precious people,
How I love you!
I see that you are trying to keep my word,
To do my will,
And I will bless you
For your efforts
Because you are my people
And I love you.

Walk forth in power
For you are empowered.
Never forget that
You have been sent.
Step out knowing
Knowing that I walk with you,
Knowing that you are my advocates.
You do not go alone
Go with confidence
Confront your fears
Or that which causes opposition.
So walk on
I am with you
You do not walk alone
We walk together
And together we can do
Whatever needs to be done.

Do not be satisfied to love
You must assure that those you love
Are aware of your care.

Leave not the word unspoken,
The act without performance.

Be clear about it -
Say it if you feel it –
The thought does not exist
If left within yourself.

Speak it out and
Give it life.

You are, indeed, a holy people,
A people of the one God.
It is a glorious thing
To be among this group,
This most holy people.

Are we not the most
Fortunate of people
To have each other?
You have your one God
And I have my people
We stand together.

PRAISE EACH OTHER

As you raise me up –
Raise your brother!
For out there is much
Suffering and pain.
You can assume this for your brother
By reaching down and raising him up,
For he suffers much.
Soften your words,
See the good, Speak it out loud..
Support his strengths
And forget his weaknesses.
Many, many will remind him of these.
This is not your job.
Your job is to raise my people up.
To overwhelm them with love,
Help them to see
The good within themselves
And the weaknesses will fall away.
Therefore, love, praise
And lift up your brother.

I am, indeed, the God of the plain,
The wind in the pines whispers My name.
The colors of the setting sun
Splash my name across the palate of the sky.
Imagine what I have prepared for you
When you look upon my works.

Majesty

God of the seas
God of the trees

Majesty

Abandon yourselves to me
For it is this whole-hearted
Response that I want from you.
No half-hearted measures will be accepted.

For you are a triumphant people
And "triumphant" is not a partial commitment,
But an extravagant
Flurry of gift of self

6/21/94

THE DELIGHT

My most precious little ones
You are my delight
Oh, how I do delight in you –
How I enjoy it
When you take a moment and remember me
At some point during the day
And when you spend a little more time with me in "quiet time".

Continue to grow in relationship with me
Walk toward me
Do not back away
For I have such wonderful delights for you
So many blessings are in store for you.
I want to pour out my blessings on you.

Many of you are here tonight to lift up another –
To bring him/her before me.

It is in your unity
That I accept this offering and bless it.

It is in your faith
That I honor the deepest desires of your heart.

For I honor the desires
Of my faithful ones.

And you are truly my beloved.
Bring your cares to me.

HAVE A GRATEFUL HEART

Have a grateful heart
For you have much to appreciate
My beautiful creation – protect it
Your fellow creatures –love them
The more you take and use with graciousness –
The more that will be given to you.

As with Israel
I suckle you at my breast
Feeding you on the milk of human kindness –
For you must look toward one another
For your support and satisfaction.

8/9/94

It is through His stripes that we are healed
And it is through our own as well
That we minister to the world.

His blood, His pain, our salvation
Our blood, our pain –
Offered up to our fellow man –

This is the method of our own redemption
As well as that of our brother.

Still your tongue!
Halt your walk
The talk is not yours
Nor is the walk –

For I have put
The spring in your step
The bend in your knee
The word to your lips
And thought in your mind.

So trust not in yourselves
For your spirit is weak
I am your stronghold
Hold on to your faith.

You are a redeemed people
You are my blessed ones
You are my holy ones

And I do count on you
I count on your ministry
To my people.

Were it not for you
I would have no voice –
Such a limited way to
Minister to my people.

Thanks to you
My word can be spread
And I can gather my people into the fold.

The time is now
It is nigh upon you

I will be with you
In a powerful way

Do not stand aside
And let me pass by

For there are many
To whom I must minister.

It is up to you
To bring my people to me
I am counting on you
Go to the highways and byways
And bring my people to me!

(For the Charismatic Conference the following week)

I am with you at all times – throughout the day

I am that knawing reminder That jogs your memory

I am that happy "coincidence"

The comment from another that builds you up

(Perhaps you cannot hear it from me)

I am that special blessed circumstance you find yourself in

I am there too, when others hurt you – I comfort you

When things go wrong I give you the insight

To seek the meaning in the situation that will help you grow.

As I told you, "I will be with you always"

And I am

I walk with you

Talk to you (through others sometimes).

I am with you always.

Your praise is my
>ice cream,
>bite of chocolate,
>angel cake!

Thank you for the treat!

Be here now...
The moment is mine
Enter into the moment,
The present –

For if you do not,
If you do not recognize my presence
With you right now – in this moment

You miss the whole point
That I am with you
Yesterday, today, and tomorrow.
(Related to a reading at Mass – the vision of the dry bones - from Ezekiel
37:14 "O my people! I will put my spirit in you that you may live...NAB)

Do not be daunted by the circumstances and obstacles before you.
I will minister to you.

Life is sweet
We were meant to be in this together.
There are rivers that flow freely and joyfully,
And barriers to be surmounted,
The mountains to be scaled,
All is good, for I made it so.
Therefore, approach all your activities and encounters
With enthusiasm, hope, peace, and love.

Yes, I am holy, and you are all holy too –
You are most precious,
I love you so much –
You are everything to me.
Allow me to show my appreciation of you.
Be open to my gifts, my blessings.
I have much to give to you.
Look at my bounty –
Who else am I to give it to but to those I love?
Take your inheritance now.
It is awaiting you.

WORDS FROM 1995

Do not concern yourselves
With the words you will speak
For my Holy Spirit within you
Speaks to the father for you.

The Spirit speaks
Of the deepest desire of your heart
And conversely, those of the Father for you
And those he has put in your path.

Attune yourselves to the voice
Of the Holy Spirit within you
So that you can be fully aware
Of yourselves, His desire for you, and for those around you.

In no way are you to believe
That I am the author of sickness.
I would never strike you down

I build up
I would never injure the holiness of your body
For it is my Temple,
My holiness within you.
You are most precious to me
Each and every part of you
Each is distinct and individual.
It saddens me when you fall
It pains me when you are hurt
I suffer your pain beside you

I build you up
Strengthen you
Shower you with my abundance.
I would never slap you down
Awaiting your pleas for help
I would not plant something malignant within you
I am the one who would pluck it out.
I do not tend suspicious toxic cells within your body
I wash them clean and flush them without
Through the waters of my salvation.

I give life.
I do not take it away
So do not let sickness
Separate you from me
This is not of me.

TONGUES

You are my most precious ones
I love you
I hold you in the palm of my hand –

If this sounds hackneyed
As if I have said it before,
It is true.

This is just the reason
That I have given you the gift of tongues.

So that we can speak together in mutual understanding
You will fully know how much I love you
And I will know your love for me without words.

BEING WITH YOU

It is not that I do not want to be in that moment of reflection
Or present at your regular prayer time
Or with you in a moment of service

Rather, it is that I want to be the wave that washes over your day,
The wind, as it whispers in your ear as you move about,
The water that, when you drink, thoroughly refreshes your body within.

I want to be continuously on your mind in your heart imprinted on your soul!

You are the blossom of my love
The seed of my Word
Open yourselves fully to others
And when the time is right
Freely sow my seed
For the world is a barren place
Stark and cold
You, my flowers
Respond and open to my light
And with the death of yourselves
It is I who am sewn.

THE DOVE RETURNS HOME

This Holy Spirit of ours -
It is an elusive thing,
It blows as it will,
Dwells where it desires.

Take care that your tree (of life)
Is always ready to receive Him
So that He will nest in your branches
Make a home and dine
Among your leaves
And will return again and again
To your waiting arms.

For it is through forgiveness
That we are set free
It is in letting go and leaving
That we arrive and begin

Come now my people...
You are becoming complacent!
Remember –

To those to whom much has been given,
Much is expected.

You have been given in abundance...
My hand is always open to you,
You are the gifted.

Let there be no concern
Among you that your cup will be refilled
As it is emptied

Distribute your wealth
(More than your money) generously

There are many among you
Who are starving –

Not for food – but for your leftovers
The leftovers you withhold

The leftovers you waste
The leftovers you have not developed
Therefore, go forth
Use what you have been given
And you will receive much more

To me you are more perfect than the structure of my snowflake
Richer than my earth that nurtures the grain –
Clearer than my rains that purify the land
You are my highest form of love, my perfection.

Put aside all else
And abandon yourselves to me.

Pause, and listen to me
Throughout your day
You will gain insights
Get direction-
Feel a warm glow within
Each time we are in touch

You do not need to
Await times like these
To experience my presence
In your everyday life

I am with you always
At all times
In all places
Reach out and touch me often

I have enjoyed your praise
And have ministered healing
To many tonight.

I minister to you
That you may minister
To the world

Go forth,
And allow my healing
To multiply
To all of my people

You are servant
Above all else,
You are servant to one another.

The Christian mission is service
Being my personhood in the world

Follow My Son
The Master Servant
The Servant of Mankind
Your Servant.

Go forth
Your ministry is the world
They are your people
And mine!

I am opportunity
I am that slight pause
Between comments
That look that anticipates more

The lingering hope
Of encouragement
The wait that invites
My entry into your presence

Function as my arteries to the world
So that I may pump my blood to the world

You are the major carriers of my salvation –
Those on the fringes (of my body) are deprived

Assure that they receive what they need for their salvation

Do not remain in your stoic positions
I exhort you to step out

Be proactive, rather than reactive
Move out of your comfort zones!

You are my ambassadors of Hope
It is through you that I inspire
It is through you that I enliven
That I encourage and give new life
It is through you
That I enable people to grow
To become that self that I have created.
They are my words in your mouth
My voice that calms,
I enable you to hear the pain,
To touch the heart,
To sense the suffering.
Therefore, I need your presence
Among my people –
I need you to "be there" for them.
Prepare yourselves
To listen, to hear,
To feel, to touch my people

IT IS YOU WHO ARE THE SAINTS

You are indeed a pure and holy people
A blessed people.

It is I who have made you so
I am raising up a people!

Continue to walk in my ways
Let me continue to
Make you holy.

(Tomorrow is All Saints Day)

[150]

WORDS FROM 1996

To the Neophytes
My people
I am pleased with your walk toward relationship with me.
Advance –for I wait for you.

To Mature Members

Gather together with your family
Bask in each other's love..
You are family
<u>My</u> family!
I hold you close to my heart –
I love you.
What I have is yours.

Do not be concerned about your imperfections
You are at the place you are at –

It is not your job – this job of perfection.
It is mine and I will take care of it.

I call you now. Follow me
Open your hearts
and I will make you into the person you were meant to be.

Do not be afraid

Do not be afraid of what I ask

For I will give you the power.

I am the evergreen of the natural forests
The crystal-clear waters from deepened springs.

The playful friskiness of the little cub.
The effervescence of your human kind.

I am the prize pedigree, I am the runt.
I am the eagle in flight, the nesting hen.

The hare, scampering in the field,
The beaver in the dam.

All living creatures, large and small
Are mine and I am theirs.

Come, join me
I spread my table of gifts
Come, partake.
I have much for you
There is an abundance
I spread it all before you.
Why do you fast and deprive yourself?
I want you to be filled with my abundances.
Why limit your selves
When you have access to all that I have?
Come, join me,
Fill yourselves with all that I have for you
First, and foremost,
My loved ones, is,
Of course, my body and blood
Which you have just received.
There is more for you,
So much more,
I pour out my blessings.
Open your hearts to receive them
I do not stint
In sharing what I have with you.
I will never stop
Showering my gifts on my people.
You are ever so precious to me...
Most precious...
My beloved.

THE FLOOD

As the floodwaters
Will not abate
I pour forth a multitude of graces.
I rush toward you
Eager to wash over you.

Receive me –
Open yourselves to me
Anticipate my arrival
Prepare yourselves
My current is strong
And awaits no one.

I wash away your sin
Your pain and troubles too
I wash you clean
And none of these shall
'er return.

Jesus Lives!
When they look into your eyes
Let them see me!

When they see your works
Let them be mine!

Be my presence in the world
Show them that Jesus Lives!

THERE ARE MANY PATHS TO THE ULTIMATE GOAL

I call you to be creative!
Find your own way to me.

There are many calls and many paths.
I enjoy variety!

Remember I blessed the
Disciple who doubled what he had been given.

The walk is not just in the goal –
It is in the process.

Yes, you are a most magnificent people.
And yes, I mean even with your sinfulness.
Yes, you are imperfect.
That part of you even makes you more
Precious to me (for then you need me).
Just think, if you will,
How you feel as parents
When your children come to you for help –
Or will even listen to you.
This is how I feel about you –
(and treat your own children this way) –
I affirm you
You are most perfect
Just as you are.
Draw closer to me,
For I want to be even nearer to you.
You are on my mind all the time.
I wait for you (consider how a parent waits to hear
from their child late at night
when they have not heard from them and are worried).
Stay close and speak to me.
Stay close and listen to me and each other.
Stay close to me –
I want to love you.
Stay close to me –
I want to hold you.
Be quiet, sit and pray with me often.
I love you so much –
More than you can ever know,
For my heart is full of you and yours.

JUST PASSING BY

Grasp your freedom
Lest it pass you by.
The Spirit blows as it will
If you do not accept it
Others will!

Be spontaneous!
Wake up! Grasp your hope!
Do it now!
I am near –
Do not let me pass you by.

The alarm sounds!

Awake! Be alert!

I am building my army of the elite.

You are elected!

You have been chosen from the beginning.

You have received enough milk -

Now is the time!

Go forth. You are ready.

I have placed my seal of approval on you.

Go forth! Do not wait!

The time is now!

And I have made you ready.

I will put the words in your mouth.

The love in your heart.

You are ready! I go with you! Go!

You are the fruit of my love

You, too, must bear fruit.

If you are barren

My vine will wither and die.

You are the flowers of my crucifixion

You blossom and flourish

Take me as your own

Taking on color, richness, and texture

As you are immersed in my blood

My life, my death, my meaning.

Image of carnations & roses that have been placed in red dye (his blood) and have turned a velvet red)

Let the sunrise
Of my compassion
Wash over you.

And at sunset
Bring your guilt to me,
Letting it wash away with the tide.

Repent and let it go.
For I wash you clean
In the waters of your baptism.

So be joyful, be elated!
For I have picked you up,
Brushed you off,
And send you on your way.

WORDS FROM 1997

4/29/97

My people
I prepare the way for you
I make straight the path.

The way is clear
If only you would discuss it
If only you seek out my way.

Mine is not always the easy path
At times it is strewn
With distraction and dilemma.

Your mind may be open to confusion, sadness
Or even despair along the way

Know, however, that I point the way.
That it is in, with, and through me
That you emerge victor!

YOU, MY COMMUNITY

I relish the variety
Of your giftedness,
And will use you in your uniqueness
To further my kingdom.

There are many ways to love:

Allowing someone to take responsibility for their behavior,

Confronting them with the truth,

Standing aside while they do some of the work themselves,

Encouraging and motivating them to follow through on their promptings.

Never forget, however, that I am there with you -

Not watching, but walking thru these circumstances together with you.

WORDS FROM 1998

You are indeed a most gifted people.

I shower you with my blessings.

Do you recognize them and express your gratitude?

If you are not experiencing my joy and peace

Ferret out the barrier between us.

It is of your making – not mine.

Despite your failings

You are most precious to me

I continue to pour out my Spirit to you – in abundance.

THE SEED

I have planted within you
Seeds of faith
Water them, fertilize them
Tend them with care
That they may flourish
And serve you well
As you go upon your way

I have gifted this community with many of the gifts of the Holy Spirit.

You must use them to: encourage each other, enliven the spirit among you

And to bring glory to my Name.

For it is thru these gifts that I mold my people

And it is thru them that you will experience my presence among you.

I am knocking at the door to your heart, laden with gifts.

I bid that you accept these,

For I choose to give to you in abundance.

DIVERSITY

Glory in your variety
For it was/is in my most creative imagination
That I have formed you.

Rejoice in your own special color, race, gender, age
For each has their own insight,
Portion to serve and will speak to certain hearts.

I relish your diversity
Your own special ways pleasure me
I have work for all – I need your differences.

Could I have created anything less
Just look at the variety of grasses, and trees...
You are so special in your differences.

WORDS FROM 1999

8/24/1999

Do not concern yourselves
With your own or the
World's imperfections.

I have called you to holiness
But love you no less
With your imperfections.

Some are even quite humorous.
I watch your efforts, your strivings
Your wish to please me and better serve your fellow man.

Take heart! It is <u>I</u> who will perfect you!
I love you with all your weaknesses
Take heart! You will grow.
Live gloriously
Live in the victory!
The important thing is to be there for me.

Cleanse yourselves,
Cleanse your vessels
Prepare yourselves for my work.

There are many among you
Who will not listen to, or
Do not recognize my voice.

I need you
I need you to be with these people.
They are in dire need.

Open yourselves to me
In order that you are
Prepared for my work.

It is all around you
Be alert! Look for me
Look for my people
Look for an opportunity
To be of service!

WORDS FROM 2000

Peace I give to you

It is your inheritance

Peace, quiet, tranquility

It is yours – but you must claim it

You must ask for it

And you must make a place

For it in your life.

Sometimes this means

To give something else up.

You must make room for me in your life.

I will not intrude

I will not insist

I will not push myself into your life.

You must make a place for me

Invite me in

And I will reside there

In the place you have made for me

And will be a great comfort to you.

I am raising up leaders among you.

When I call – respond.

I will give you the words and the power.

Respond - act!

Put the faith that you have into action.

I go before you

I go with you

You sow the seed

I will water it

And enable it to grow.

You have much to offer

Your fellow man/woman

Hearken my people!

The time is neigh

Live your lives as though

These were the end times.

(And indeed it is – in many ways

For soon my Son will present himself

The end times are not much different).

In the end you will see the Father

During this time you will see my Son manifest himself.

You are truly blessed

For you already know me through my son and Holy Spirit

Your spirit often rests with me

Your heart recognizes me, knows me

And we are friends.

WORDS FROM 2001

My people

Each of you has a contribution to make.

You may be concerned that it is small,

But in union with others

It can be a powerful force for good

If each contribute to the larger work

Together we will prevail!

2/20/01

Look to my Son
In Whom I am well pleased (Matthew 17:5)
He has shown you The Way
The path of holiness.
Quietly minister to those
Among you who are vulnerable.
Be patient with these who may not
Be as quick as you.
Give until it is uncomfortable.
Walk in peace, dismiss violence.
Reach out your arms in graciousness
To the stranger and the poor.
Be patient with those slower than you –
Love those difficult to love, the irritating.
Serve those who lift you up.
Not all paths lead to me
Stay focused on me –
Of one heart and mind,
Follow Him, my most precious Son.
He knows the way.

THE GIFT

I have poured out my gifts to you with abandon.
Who among you would not lift them high for all to see?
Who would not thank the giver?
Accept and use what I have given.

Which of you would put my gift on the shelf to gather dust?
Who would put it away in a corner to rest from disuse?
Our gifts only expand with use – they grow and become fine-tuned.
Only then are our gifts mature.

HOPE

Do not grow weary
My workers in the vineyard.
There is too much for you to be doing.
Do not give up hope – for none are lost
My people must know
That there is hope for them
Hope that it is not too late to change
To come to me.

Quiet yourselves, be still,

For my presence inhabits the quiet soul.

Stop flitting around taking care of everyone else's business.

Take care of our business,

Be still.

How can we conduct our business amid chaos?

Sit down, be with me –

I want to speak to your heart.

This is the heart's business,

Not the worlds'

There is much to do between us

First we must tend to you –

Only then will you be of help to others.

You must fill yourselves,

Only then is there plenty for others.

Come to me my people

And be filled.

COME, I WILL LIFT YOU UP

Do you find yourselves entrenched in the world?

    Come, I will lift you up.

Are you easily irritated, trapped in the trivia of the world?

    Come, I will lift you up.

Do you hunger for more – dissatisfied with the gifts of the world?

    Come, I will fill you up.

Does the world offer you little more than continual frustration?

    Come, I will lift you up.

I will fill your cup to overflowing

    What you yearn for will be yours – and more.

My gifts hold no limit

    Copious and freely given,

I will pour them out on you

    And it is only you who

Limit my generosity

    Reach out your hands and ask –

I will give it –

    I am a giver

All you need to do is open your hearts and receive.

FOR I AM A GOD OF LOVE

Whatever it is that results in love
I bless
That that results in peace
I bless
Actions whose ends are kindness
I bless
Walk my way
And your behavior will reflect me
And I will bless you
For I am a God of love –
And these are the fruits of my way.

Come,
Grow along with me –
I have shown you the path
I walk before you
Do not fear
I am with you always.

Do not act as if you are unaware
Do not be unsure
I have put my seal upon you
You are marked as my own
So walk with assurance.

I ask much of you
But you are equipped
Do not be afraid!
What is there to fear?
For I am with you

The world cannot say as much
They labor alone
It is not so between us
For we have each other.

WORDS FROM 2002

Much of the world is dry and barren
There is little to nurture us or quench our thirst
It is you, therefore, who must be my river
Flowing out among my people, flowing from me

You must be firmly rooted, rich in fruit
Kind and loving to yourselves
So that you bear with abundance

Love yourselves, forgive yourselves
Love each other, forgive each other
And your giftedness will flow forth
In a running stream
(Received during song: His Peace is Flowing Like a River)

It brings great joy to my heart
That you prepare a place for me
Among yourselves
In much the same way that
I prepare a place for you
In the heavens
I see you preparing a place for me
Within your hearts
And in your lives
A mother bird gathers
Only the choicest bits
Of feather, moss, and twigs
The wild thing, like the wolf
Secures a dry place
Safe and out of the way
You cannot imagine
The elation I feel
At your invitation to me
I will snuggle into
The place you
Have made for me

And remain there
For you have made
A place for me today
In your hearts and lives

UNITY: MY ARMY

You are not alone
       You are my people
"People" do not
       Function independently
They join together and are
       Of one heart and mind.
You do not minister
       Independently
You carry with you myself
       And the faith of those within the community
Together we enlighten
       Teach
       Heal broken hearts
We enhance people's lives
       We speak to them
We let them lean
       On us for support
We pray for them
       We help them on their way
Together we have great strength
       Much wisdom
       Understanding
       Insight
Never fear that you go out alone
       On my mission
Lean on me and each other
       We are here for each other
The whole
       Gathered together
Mighty and Grand -
       My army

WORDS FROM 2003

Stand up!

Be stalwart!

If not you, who will it be?

Whom can I send?

If you will not carry my message

Who will do it?

It is you I have chosen –

Now be there for me.

I rely on you, touch my people

Speak my words to them –

Just be my presence to them.

You are my hope, you are the hope of my people

For it is often that through your ministries

That my people are brought to me.

Take heart –

For you often stand among the thorns

And may feel contaminated by the evil surrounding you.

But recall

There was one before you

Who found himself in that position too.

Do not recoil

Leaving them to their own devices

For many among them do not know how to choose rightly.

Without you

Where might they turn?

To whom might they go?

For it was this for which I came –

To be present among you

Especially when you are not at your best.

Healed!

Of course I want you healed!

What kind of witness are you

Walking around with a long face, depressed?

Critical natures are more than unpleasant,

They are inconsistent with a Christian's inner life.

More is required of you

My glory must shine from you,

Internally to externally

How can faith be manifest in a dirty vessel?

And hope! How can you exhibit this

When you have no trust in our history?

Be healed?

Of course!

Prepare yourselves inwardly

The truth, then, cannot fail but to exhibit

My glory – my healing.

Let me purify you
Individually
For some this may be
To spur you to action.
To others it may be
To quiet you down for some time with me.
It may be to serve that neighbor
You have in need.
It could be to daily mass.
Perhaps community service,
Or learning discipline through
Honoring the little things.
You may have the opportunity to witness
Or visit someone in the hospital,
Or babysit for someone who needs to get away.
Open your mind and heart to
Whatever opportunity occurs in your life
Be there for me when I cannot be,
Serve your fellow man,
Be with me,
Wait,
Act,
I will lead you in what direction to take.
Each of you will be called
According to your giftedness
Whatever your call
Do not fear,
For I will bless your call
And be there with you.
I will call when the other is ready to receive.
Be there for me
Be there for them.
Be there for your own personal growth in the Spirit.

Prepare yourselves!
I have work for you to do!
Make a place for me
In your lives to hear my word.

Take time for me.
Make ready your body and
Your minds,
For I have much for you to do

You are my laborers
The work is not easy
You must make the time.
It will not come to you easily.

Do not become complacent
I will work with you
I will provide the words for you
The strength you must provide
For yourselves.

Eat well,
Get some rest,
Read my Word –
Prepare –

(Easter week)

4/22/13

This remains a time of preparation
Ready yourselves
I need you
My people thirst.

Read Scripture
Fast
Use your gifts
Get ready

I want your full commitment

Be not half-hearted.

Say "yes" to each challenge

Presented to you!

The directions and decisions you

Make in daily life

Translate or correspond to

The directions and decisions you

Make in walking the walk with me.

Make time for me in your life

I want prime time!

Make me second to none,

For you are always first with me.

My people
Do not stand by impotent
And let opportunities to minister
Pass you by
You are not a weak frail people –
You carry my strength within you
You are strong
And competent people
Committed and loyal
Filled with a Christian character
Step out
You have an inner strength
You can carry on
Long after others falter
I fill you with my courage
My faith
My strength
Walk forward my chosen ones
You are stronger than you think
I am within you.

Harken my people!
Listen!
There is something here for you tonight!
Be open –
Some of what you hear you may eagerly accept –
Some may not be so palatable
And some you may have denied until now.

My voice is truth
Listen keenly
Take what is yours and own it –
Thus you will have taken the first step toward me
The truth –
I will walk with you as you respond –
And hope you will take action

To change those thing in your life
That hinder your spiritual progress
And movement toward me.
And that is not the all of it –
It harms you not to know the truth.
Facing the truth is facing me –
And do not fear

I am soft toward you.
I love you unconditionally
Step forth.

(Jer 29:11-15 For I know well the plans I have in mind for you to give you a future full of hope)

THE FRUIT OF JOY

Do not be sad,

Feel hopeless and alone.

I am the God of joy

And as you walk my path

It will burst forth,

Bubble up, spew forth,

Falling not only on yourself,

But everyone nearby.

I want to be in communion with you my people
Not only in those still, silent moments when we are alone
But in those unexpected comments of your neighbors
Recognize me.
Recognize my voice
Yes, also in the critique you receive – it is my correction
In a musical lyric or rhyme
Recognize me
Recognize my voice

Where you find the truth you find me
Keep the space around you holy
So that others recognize that I am around,
Lingering in the spaces
Those who know me recognize me
Those who may not yet know me
Will begin to see that I live here
With you
Among you
In you.

WORDS FROM 2004

Do not discredit

The means others

May find as their way to me.

I am a God large enough for all.

The important thing is the search –

That they seek to know me.

It may well be that

Their imagination and creativity

May stretch your own faith,

And you may be the instrument I will use

To further enlighten others in their search.

I have placed my angels – my sentinels around you –

Around the prayer group

Separating you from the world tonight.

Speak out words of encouragement, comfort to each other

Do not concern yourselves with how it will sound

Do not fear – you are surrounded with those who love you.

Speak out – your gift is for the upbuilding of the community

Touch each other

Speak your love and caring

Be there for each other.

Fear not!

I go before you

Behind you

And walk beside you

There is much work to do

It is already planned for you

All I need is your acceptance

You are my workers in the vineyard.

Do not be idle

If not you, who??

Yes, you have made this place holy -

Your presence here evokes my presence, thus it is holy –

Wherever you go during the day

It is the same –

You r presence blesses that location

You bring me with you

Assure that you are aware of this

And keep yourselves holy –

Be holy vessels.

(After singing "Surely the Presence of the Lord is in this Place")

Have a gracious, grateful spirit

And speak it out!

For it is through this attitude

That you speak of my unconditional love

Tell the world what it is that I have given you

Tell it that you depend on me

That I gift you abundantly

And you have much left over to share

And you can afford to be gracious, kind,

Understanding, and compassionate

For this has been given to you in abundance

Be grateful, for you have much to be grateful for

You have been given much

You have the entirety of my heart

Like Mary,

There are things you treasure in our heart –

Things difficult to speak of

Sometimes small, seemingly inconsequential things

Inconsequential, perhaps, to some

But things of great value to you

Things that may have created turning points in your life –

But things I have given you

That may even have been surprises to you –

See how creative and imaginative I am...

I know you, I know your heart, I know your needs

Even though you may not know them yourself.

Share them with each other tonight,

It helps to build my community.

Oh that you were aware of my presence among you

That you would open your ears and eyes

For I am present to you

Like a feather brushing against your lips

When I would have you speak

In a whisk of a breeze upon your ear

That you would listen.

Be attentive, my children, and you will receive

Insights known only to me and the heart that suffers.

You will know, and experience, share,

The pain that your fellow man tells no one.

In this way others will know

My compassion and my desire to

Shoulder their cross with them

And you will recognize my presence

With you throughout the day.

Soar –

I want you to soar –

You were not meant to be

Tethered to the earth –

You were meant to soar –

I have equipped you

To lift yourselves up from your earthly cares.

Can you not see

That I lift you up?

I want you to fly free

I blow the wind among your wings.

Just spread your wings

It will be effortless

For I lift you through and above

Life's hurdles

I lift you up – now

(Imagine a dove flying over the earth)

Killing, violence, evil
Surround you
To counteract it
You must pray
Not only pray
But perform good works

The world must observe
Your good works
Perhaps it is not possible
For it to be publicized
Much like the war,
Or various acts of theft,
Muggings and assaults.
It will, however,
Be magnified in His eyes,
And as you witness
The good that you see
The Spirit will spread
The word
And tell the world of your good deeds.
Counteract evil with good.
Do not wait –
Pray and act now.

Mine is more than a gentle thrust in the direction

I would have you go -

You will know exactly when I prompt you

I will urge you

There will be no doubt

As to the author of the call

The Spirit within you

Will recognize me

Your response must be

"Is it I Lord?

I am ready to serve

I offer myself to you

Use me as you will

Here I am Lord".

As the early morning dew

Settles on each blade of grass

I rest upon you, as you are still and await my touch.

I will refresh you, as I alight on you

I will wash you clean

I will remove what is old, tired, and useless to you

(such as your fears, concerns, worries)

I want to free you up,

Restore your faith,

Refresh your spirit

Renew our love,

Our commitment to each other

So that you can start again afresh

Each day – a new creation.

GIVE ME THE OPPORTUNITY

I do not demand your love,
Your commitment to do my work in the world.
I do not tell you what to do and when to do it
But I do suggest – ask you sometimes –
To plant the seed.

Some of you choose to go hapless along your way
Thinking endlessly about your own lives – preoccupied –
So that the weary among you,
The hopeless, the dependent and needy
Walk quietly by outside of your awareness.

Would that you would but open your eyes,
Ask questions, listen,
See what is before you, behind you, alongside you.
Then pay attention to my promptings
I will give you the words
I will speak to my people's hearts
I will comfort them
Stand with the
Listen to them
Fill them with my love,
Wisdom, and understanding. ----
If you but give me the opportunity.

I provide in abundance

Do not stint, therefore, in your giving

Do it joyfully, open-handedly.

Offer; do not wait for others to ask,

Press it assuredly, insistently into their palms,

Ignore their protestations, it is justifiably theirs.

You are but a keeper of this world's wealth

Distribute yours to those in need,

For in reality it is theirs.

Let me make it simple –

I am your focus –

Keep your eyes on me.

Do not allow yourself to be distracted.

Think clearly, simply, and speak concisely,

Without flourish.

Those will hear you

Whose eyes and ears I have opened.

Do not concern yourself with your audience

I speak through you

Into their minds and hearts.

Open yourselves to my bounty

For I have many gifts ready to bestow.

WORDS FROM 2005

Imagine, if you will, the early morning sun
    Peeking from its nighttime route
All crimson and yellow, spewing its rays,
    Pushing itself out for the day.

Imagine the dew and light puffy fog
    Being coached atop the ground.
This is how my Holy Spirit rests on you –
    Surrounding, yet lightly clinging.

Do not allow this conference to be
But a gesture
Of your love toward me.

Prepare yourselves by prayer and fasting
Gather my people
Let this be a mighty wave
To wash the face of the earth
Bring my people to me.

WORDS FROM 2006

We are to be like islands among the chaotic world,

Manifesting love, peace, generosity,

Kindness, patience, and all the other fruits of the Holy Spirit.

Be quiet in the world.

Be comforted my children
I feel your sorrows, pain, troubles.
Be assured that I shoulder your situation with you.

Never fear that you walk alone –
That you confront the world by yourself.
Know with certainty
That I would never abandon you.

Walk directly ahead,
With certainty,
With the knowledge
That I walk beside you.

Adhere, my children, to the laws and traditions

Handed down by your forefathers.

For they are rich in wisdom and well tested.

These organize and structure your lives,

Give it meaning.

When you have fulfilled these responsibilities and obligations

You are free to be creative.

(At Adoration –Adoration theme was God's abundant love)

My people!

How many times must I repeat –

You are a new creation!

You must act like one!

You must act the part!

Put on the mantle!

Remember, my yoke is easy,

My burden, light. (Matthew 11:30)

What is the good of a new inner self

If your garment on the outside is stained?

Reach inside, touch

And fondle the new little creation

I have put inside you

Much like you would fondle an infant.

What do people do with infants?

They coo, talk softly and sweetly.

This is how you are to talk to your new and vulnerable self

Be kind to yourself, and gentle, as with a babe.

And has science not shown that the more positive attention

And touching an infant receives,

The healthier they develop?

Let me help you to know and love yourself

From the inside out.

Look, feel, talk nicely to yourself

And low and behold

What will you find?

That most perfect seed that I have planted in each of you –

Look for it, water it, fertilize it

And you will see

All that I have in mind for you,

But remember, you must care for it

For it is fragile, just like an infant.

You must hold the infants' head

Until it can do it itself

You must wash and bathe it

Until it can care for itself.

It must stumble & fall

Until it can walk,

Make choices, and decisions.

So take care my children,

You have been made a new creation

Take care of yourselves and thrive!

WORDS FROM 2007

Oh, my children

     How I long to be with you.

Oh, my children

     But to take you aside.

Oh, my children

     You are mine. I claim you!

Look not ahead, or behind

     For I walk with you, now, in this moment.

Do not lament what has passed

     Or long for what is yet to be

For mine is the present moment

     I await your presence

I cherish you

     Come be with me.

You are the salt of the earth
As such, you bring out the flavor
Of each ingredient in the dish I have created.

You are like the conductor of my orchestra,
Refining each tone produced,
Like a physical trainer,
Defining each muscle, of perfecting human form.

I send you out among my people
Observe, assess, and help them to be
All that they can be –
I have placed you where I want you to be.

You are the church!
Enter into the process of your spirituality.
No more looking on from the outside.
Grow together,
My church is built from within,
You are its heart.

I have placed the seed of belief within your heart
This community and those who love you
Have developed and nurtured its growth
Until it is now mature.

Wait no longer
You are prepared
Now is the time –
Do not be afraid
You are ready

Hasten forth, do not delay
For the earth is arid and barren
Know that it awaits my outpouring
As one fasting welcomes each precious drop of water offered.

SACRIFICE?

What kind of sacrifice do I seek from you?

Time to wait with me

The time to care for your neighbor

To "accidently" drop a bill on the ground for one in need

The grace and patience to continue to listen

When one needs someone to understand.

To serve when you have already emptied yourself

This I ask of you.

Sacrifice

Then tell no one using this method.

When you come to me at the end of the day

You lay before me the best of yourselves.

STAND UP AND BE COUNTED

There are issues on the table
Within your community at large
Decisions to be made –
Actions to take –

Remember when I confronted
The money-changers in the temple?
There are times when you, too,
Must take a stand.
That time is now.

Directions need to change
Stand up!
Stop standing in the gray
Be passionate!

Remember my passion for you
Don't waver!
Do it now!

There are those among us tonight
Who are uneasy with this new experience.
Sit back, relax, be open
To the word of encouragement from others,
To Scripture,
Interpretation of the Word.
Sing praise – enter into the praise
I live in your praises
Be here now
Wait with me
Be here now

11/27/07

Let my children come unto me
I have led them,
Prompted them to gather ever closer.
They need stand alone no longer
For they enter into family –
My church
They are home now
They can relax,
Be themselves
Knowing they are loved
Just as they are.

WORDS FROM 2008

Be teachable –

Humble yourselves to one another –

Submit to correction –

Give correction –

Ask for discernment –

Don't wait to be asked –

You have the tools –

Talk to each other and listen –

For if you listen to each other keenly

You will hear me

Working through each of you.

I seek vessels to speak my direction, care,

And longing to be close to you,

Present in your heart.

Peace
Peace I leave to you
Assure that those around you
Are also left with peace.

I am not an angry God
Do not be an angry people

I have shown you patience
Now show patience to your fellow man.
Be generous and kind
See my generosity toward you
Be gracious to each other
For you have seen what I have done for you.

Your life may not always be comfortable and free of pain,
It may be heavy laden, a place where suffering has lain.

4/8/08

GIVE ME THE OPPORTUNITY

I will not <u>demand</u> your love,

Your commitment to do my work in the world.

I do not tell you what to do and when to do it

But I do suggest – ask you sometimes –

To plant the seed.

Some of you choose to go haplessly along your way

Thinking endlessly about your own lives - preoccupied –

So that the weary among you,

The hopeless, the dependent and needy

Walk quietly by outside of your awareness.

Would that you would but open your eyes,

Ask questions, listen,

See what is before you, behind you, alongside you.

Then pay attention to my promptings

I will give you the words

I will speak to my people's hearts

I will comfort them

Stand with them

Listen to them

Fill them with my love,

Wisdom, and understanding.

---If you but give me the opportunity.

I have set my tent among you
I have planted my heart.
Concern yourselves not with
What, how much, or when you should give,
For the well is deep, wide, and abundant.
Be not concerned, for what I have is yours.

Today look for:

Keep open your eyes to see

Your ears to hear

And your heart to understand

And you will see me throughout your day

Be aware

Be awake!

Be mindful

Do not pass me by today and ignore me.

WORDS FROM 2009

MY GODLY PEOPLE

You are my inheritance to the world.

You are the goodness planted there.

You are that small corner where one can be at peace.

You may be that one small hope that someone hangs on to.

Who will bring the joy if not you?

Where will one find rest if not with you?

Who will my people find to talk to,

To listen,

To understand,

If not you?

Is there no one?

Then let it be you to take my light into the world.

You are here tonight – this weekend -
Because you felt my call and responded
Many hear my call and ignore it
Despite my many efforts to reach some
They have no time for me.
I am so elated that you
Turned to face me
When I called.
Now I have your attention
And can teach you
Be attentive students.
Know that I exult
Over your presence
What joy it brings to my heart.
You are most precious to me –
Like rare stones –
Walk closer toward me
Come closer
Now that you recognize me
I am so in love with you!
(From Life in the Spirit Seminar)

Have courage my children!
It is not my intent
To send you on stressful missions.
I send you, I insist on you,
Because I know that in your heart that you are willing.

You may not feel you are ready
But I urge you to be my helpmate on this
I have no other.
I know it is difficult for you to understand
But the need is great.

It is time to start giving back
There are too many in your area
Who do not know me,
Who have not had your experience
Of my unconditional love, who feel unloved

Unworthy of love in any form
They have learned not to trust in love.
Oh, but they have never known me.
Because to know me
Is to be loved.
You are a lover because you have known me
Your job is to enable others to know me too
I will give you the energy,
Words, and courage to do it
Walk on in my love.

My children

Do not be impatient

Your timing is not my timing.

Timing is often of the essence –

The difference between success and defeat.

Often time is needed for preparation –

To prepare the earth (or heart) for the planting

The earth (and heart) must yield,

Give up its control,

Give up its environment

In order for the sower

To have an acceptable

Field for the planting.

Old ways must be dug up and aerated

Fresh air inhaled.

(the Holy Spirit must be able to breathe new life into the old)

Stand aside and let me be God

Let me take over –

Just be ready to lend a hand

When I say so.

(After St. Francis' Day of Recollection)

My children,
Do not present a weary face to the world
As you go about my work.
If you are filled with the Holy Spirit
You are filled with joy! You are gifted!
You are loved unconditionally!
I pour out my heart to you!
Do not share it grudgingly
Give what you have been given freely
You have in abundance!
I do not stint with you.
You are filled with my Spirit.
My blood surges through you.
Have you never heard your heart beat?
It is alive!
You have life in you!
You have me
I fill you to overflowing
You are my love.
I love you without restraint.
You are my all.

My children,
I am delighted, elated
At your response to my call.
I was spontaneous, open and eager
For us to know each other better.

It is good to affiliate with my church
And others I have chosen.
Because there will be a time
When these of my children
Are those to whom you must turn.

Primarily, however, will be the relationship
You establish with me.
Alone, together we must know
That the other is willing to listen
And share their innermost selves.

Relationships are not developed overnight
We must be able to sit together,
Not speaking, just being together.
Talk is not of the essence, nor is listening.
Being together – Being present to each other
Is complete enough in itself.

You don't need the words to love me
You don't need to explain yourself.
I know all there is to know of you
Learn to know my voice, my ways,
And you will recognize me everywhere.

When you recognize me in others
It will be so easy for you to love them
Because you will know their heart.
When you love my people
You love me
And are better able to love them
As they are (as I love you).

When you learn to love others
Wholly and completely
You will know me.
Learning to love the unlovable
You put on Christ
And learn to love unconditionally.

As I have loved you,
You must love
I will teach you,
Ask for my help to love
And I will teach you.

WORDS FROM 2010

1/12/10

Close your eyes –

Gather together my people and rest.

Be at peace with yourself and the world.

I am not a God of chaos and confusion

I am quiet and at rest

Do not stir up conflict among yourselves

But accept graciously what is put before you.

I am as the mist as it hovers over the lea

If you call upon me I will cover your anxieties

With a blanket of calm

While you rest beneath

Breathe slowly and deeply

For I will fill you with peace

Beyond anything you can understand.

Many are called,
Few are chosen.
Make the most of your gifts
Of what you are given.

A NEW BEGINNING

My little chickadees
My babes
Never think that this is an ending.

It is a beginning
We are introduced.
I look forward to activities we will participate in together.
Sharing reflections together
You need to continue this
Find persons and places to do this.
Be with me alone regularly.

It is through your togetherness, your unity,
That my power flows.

Individually you are gifted,
Together you are much more.

Remember, you are greater than the sum of our parts
Together we pass on my work.

WORDS FROM 2011

My people

You are, indeed, a sweet and kind people,

I see your efforts to be holy and applaud them –

The method is not correct, however –

"Efforts" is the perfect word for it.

It is not your, yourselves,

Who will complete the task

It is me, working through you,

- that is how we get the job done.

Be alert my people!
I am calling you forth.
You who are prepared
Know who you are –
You may not be in your comfort zone
But we cannot afford to wait too long
You are being healed from the inside out
There is no such thing as being completed
You will always be in the process.
Only know that I go
Before you,
After you
Beside you
And with you
I am committed to you
You are my arms and legs, hands and feet –
I am always there for you
Now be there for me
I need you now!
Right now!

SUFFER WELL

You may create your own suffering (smoking)
You may invite the evil one into your life (occult)
I may send it as a lesson
No matter the source
Its significance lies only
In how you suffer
Much like how you die
I suggest you live, love, suffer and die well
It's your choice
Choose well.

Do you think I do not know what pain is?

My passion and death

Are but a minuscule part of what I know of it.

Can you not see that I feel not only for you, but with you?

This is my compassion.

Could I have healed the bleeding woman without feeling the power leave me?

Did I not admit to despair when I questioned if God had forsaken me?

When I cast out demons was I not required to confront the evil within?

I have known pain

Do I not know disappointment?

I was disappointed in you when you fell asleep

Don't think that I do not understand –

That I do not know,

I know

I understand

I have compassion for you

I have walked in your shoes

My heart has broken too

Experience your pain

Walk through it

Do not stop short

of the victory.

PREPARE A PLACE FOR ME

Take care of yourself

Do only that which is good for you.

Entertain nothing foreign to Me in your body.

I want a holy place,

I want to make my abode within you.

You must prepare a place for me

As a mother bird feathers its nest.

I am coming to dwell within you.

Ready yourselves for a guest......

The Comforter.

Oh my people
Follow my precepts
For they are in place for a reason
And for your best interests
They lead you to me
They prepare you

Your job for the next eight weeks
Is to be my loving presence
In the place where you live.

Listen, speak little, touch lovingly, often.
Reason, discern, then act.
Know that you are not always right –

Look at another perspective
Affirm the good, let go of the rest.
Encourage the hopeless, defend the underdog
"Be there" for your loved ones.

Be part of the solution, not part of the problem.
Say a kind word to those who need support
These are my people – they need you.

You are worthy
They are worthy.

I want to use you
Be prepared!
I have gifted you with all kinds of tools
Now be bold!
You are not to be milk-fed anymore
Grow up, be responsible for, and use
That which has been given to you
It is more than enough.
Have I not told you that I would give you the words –
And have I not told you that
Those who believe –
Who have the faith – will be healed?
Sometimes others do not know how to ask
Asking for others is no task
It is easy to ask for them
Sometimes you must ask for them.
You must prepare them for this possibility –
    That I will fill their needs.
You must present the vision
You must verbalize the hope
You must show them the way
That there is a way –
Present as holy
You represent me
Be holy for I am holy
And my spirit dwells within you

Welcome, my little ones
Welcome to my home.
To be a member of my family
You must be invited
You are adopted
I have adopted you
I have chosen you
I have called you forth
To be with me
I am the Lord
You are my hands and feet
I need you
We have much to do
I love you as my own
You are being groomed
To further my cause
To evangelize the world –
If you will not do it
Who will?
I called
You answered
You responded
Now hearken to my call
Be there for me
Our people need you

You are indeed mine

I have called,

You you answered,

You responded when you heard my voice

You have prioritized me

In order to participate in this program

But remember, it is I who first called you

Learn to recognize my voice

I want to communicate with you

I want to further my relationship with you

WORDS FROM 2012

Know that fear has no place in your lives

You must stand up and be present to me

Spend as much time listening to me

As you do talking

For you have much to learn

And I have much for you to do

You must be strong and confident in me

Know that I am behind you in all that you do in my name

Perform not for the world but to honor me

Tonight you lift me up
I bask in your praise
Now – consider each other
I challenge you.
You must also lift each other up

If not you – who will do it?
Recall right now
When was the last time
Someone gave you some encouragement?
Gave you a pat on the back?
When did they recognize your gift and thank you?

You must praise each other too –
Confirm the good works of another
Listen to your neighbor
Encourage them
Empty your pockets

And share yourselves with each other
Raise each other up
Tell each other how
Much they mean to you
Your brothers and sisters
Will bask in your praise too, as I do.

May you always remember that I am your God

Exalted above all else

I, and only I must be your focus

Other persons or projects

May compete with or interfere

And may even be time well spent

But never forget that

I am your destination

Your home

As I taught you to pray – you must sacrifice.

First, be willing to work hard to toil in my fields

The grounds are barren lest you plow the earth –

Open it up to receive me.

While it is open

Place carefully each seed

Within it and cover it

Protecting it

Water it generously

And fertilize it –

Nurture it

Feed the hungry

When you make a special dish share it

Not only with your family,

But with someone who has an empty stomach.

Share your time –

Not only your spare time,

But stop and give yourself when you are interrupted.

Assure the uncertain

When you buy a bottle of water for yourself

Give one to a person who has been on the street all day.

Make that telephone call to rectify a relationship.

Buy somebody that hat you thought looked just like them

Bring peace to a volatile situation.

Watch your plant burst from the womb and make its

Way toward the sun amid stems and flourishing leaves.

First the bud, then the bloom, beautiful as it is,

Only to die.

3/27/12

Heed my voice my people

I am constantly reaching out to you

I need you, my people, need you

But you must be alert

To my prompting

Familiarize yourselves with my voice

Come to know me

As I know your hearts.

As we come to know each other

We will appreciate each other

And love each other more.

As you let me into your daily lives

We will grow together

And become one in the Spirit.

4/3/12

Grow my little ones, grow
You are a mature community
    You are fully gifted
You have been filled, most of you
    For many years now
When will you step out
    To do my work
When will you be ready
    The time for being timid is past
You are not a floundering, young community
    That continues to ask questions.
By now you must have
    Some of the answers
I have fed you on pap
    And protected you
Now is the time to step out
    In my name
And with my support
    Into unsure waters
There is so much to do
    Come forth - I need you
Be there for me
    As I have been there for you
As a community
    I want you to step outside your comfort zone
You know me, I am a familiar voice
You trust me, you are filled
You are mature
    You have read my word, studied it

Discussed it among yourselves,
> You are ready

If not now, when
> I call you forth

I am raising my army

(Response to Ranaghan's 1991 word from "In the Power of the Spirit")

My people –

But that you knew the love I have for you

The countless blessings

I shower upon you

I do wonder, sometimes

If you are even aware –

If you recognize me in the moment

Behind the scenes

Even if it is so

That my focus is on you

More often than yours is on me

I, like any parent, love to please you

I love to see you enjoy my gifts

I love to see your face light up

With my unexpected appearance in your life

I love to be near you

You are everything to me

You are my delight

Oh my most precious ones,

Hearken to my call

I continue to call you forth

You must listen to me

Do not tire of my voice

It is expansive, but

Remember, it never returns void

I am present through my Word

Speak it, and I am with you

My word

You are my vessels

I tire of the repetitiveness of my message

When I see no movement

I pour out my message to you

I bless you abundantly

And yet nothing, nothing, zero

You are immovable

You do not respond

Where are you, my people?

Yes, my people
I am a forgiving God
However –
I have clear expectations of you
You are no longer children
You are mature Christians
How much longer must I call you forth?
I have assured you
That I will stand beside you
That I will give you the necessary words
You know my voice
I will speak loudly and distinctly
There should be no question in your minds
As to my focus –
The call to evangelization
You are such an integral part of my plan
You are my hands and my feet
You are my voice
I depend on you

I CALL YOU FORTH FROM YOUR TOMBS

I love each and every one of you
It was my call that brought you forth here tonight
Do not perceive this as insignificant
Or as something instigated by you
Because it is I who call you forth
You responded.

Consider this as a step forward
Be ready for the next and the next
As I call you out of isolation
And into relationship with me
Come forth and be in union with me
John 11:43 (Lazarus)

Remember, my children

Who you are

Remember who you are

Never forget that I suffered and died for you

I suffered and died to give you life!

Live it to the fullest

Do not stint

Live your life!

It is my gift to you

And to all mankind –

What joy you bring to my heart
My faithful servants
I stir up my Holy Spirit among you –
I enhance your giftedness
I flood you with my power
Ask and you will receive
Expect and it will be given to you
You will minister
As if I am among you
Because where you are
Where you gather together
Because where you
I am present
And in a powerful way
Step out
Test your powers in the Holy Spirit
And you will find me –
Fully present
Pray in intercession
Lay on hands
And you will observe
The glorious power of your God!
Each has his/her song to sing
Gifts distinctly their own
Each has a beauty of its own
Yet
When we join together
We make an orchestra
Something over and above
Our joint song

Listen, my people, listen

Or how will you know my voice?

Listen and ponder

Then, the next step,

Do not keep it to yourself

For my word is meant

To carry out my mission

To evangelize

To reach others

Who do not know me

Spread my word

My people
And you are my people
I claim you
You have been bought
Through my blood
I adopted you
You are mine
My blood is your blood
What is mine is yours
We share
Come forward my little ones
And claim what is yours
You have been bought
At a great price
Do not underestimate
The value of your inheritance
What is mine is yours
Claim it
Make it your own
Your inheritance is vast
Take at least some part of it
And make it your own
Personalize it
Put your stamp on it
I want to be part of you

My people,

You are so precious to me

You are my delight

I love to watch your efforts to please me –

       The drug clinics –

       The Right to Life –

       The music –

       To lead the meeting –

       To speak to someone new –

       To comfort when there's been a loss –

       And one of the members of my body is wounded –

You are my affirmers

Help my people to forgive

Help them to repent when they go another way

Teach them to pray

Teach them the way

Take the lead.

Guide my people to me.

You know the truth

You know the way to me

Others search –

I have gifted you.

Why do you hesitate?

I know you are few now

Nevertheless, I have equipped you

You know the way

Bring my children

Home to me

WORDS FROM 2013

A CHILD OF GOD

Never, ever consider
That you are anything
Other than mine.
I have claimed you
I have loved you
You are mine
And belong to no other
This cannot be a one way relationship
You must commit to me as well
I need your whole focus
I must be your priority
I must mean everything to you
No "wait a few minutes",
"Soon" or "later"
I need "right now"
I need everything
All of you
No distractions
What more can one ask for
Than a committed relationship?
And I am asking for that –
Tonight, Here, Now
Who are you?
How do you identify yourself?
Know this
Most importantly –
You are <u>Mine!</u>

My children,
I call you forth

Again, I call you forth
I continue to call you forth.
Is there a response?
I fail to see it
Either individually
Or together as a group.

What are you as a Christian
If not an evangelizer?
Where is your focus?
Observe my ministry –
To preach, teach, heal,
Remove evil where it is found
Who have you taught this week?
Have you laid hands on someone?
Have you guided someone
From the clutches of the evil one?
Have you told at least one person of me?
I challenge you
To be all that you can be
To be a real Christian
To live up to your name.

I love each and every one of you individually

I was born for you

I lived for you

I died for you

Now you must walk the walk

Walk the way I walked

With peace, kindness, patience, goodness,

Humility, gentleness, self-control

Over all on put on love

This way you will live for me

In the way I intended

And I will love you

Through it all

And that will be enough

For both of us

Today, my children,

Is a new day for you

You have been washed clean

You start anew,

Your souls as white as snow

And yes,

I will continue to feed

And nurture you

With my bread of life

Return again and again

I want to remain close to you

You hold a special place

In my heart.

Come, my children,

Come closer to me.

Together we are a mighty force.

When I was with you

I was both human and divine

Since, I am divine

And rest on you to provide

My human component

I will lift you up

You must bring me down

You, my church, must be my humanity

I, your divinity.

Small in number

But mighty in the Word

That is who you are.

Recall my few apostles

Who spread the Word

Throughout the world.

You must be to your community

What they were to the world

Go, and spread the Word,

Go, my beloved

Go in my name.

The time nears (Pentecost) when you will be renewed in the Holy Spirit.

Expect – be expectant –

Know that your gifts will be enhanced.

Ask to be filled to capacity for

I give in abundance.

Ask

If you speak in Tongues

Pray to also receive the Interpretation of Tongues.

If you Heal in my name

Ask for a Word of Knowledge.

If you are in Leadership

Ask for Wisdom & Understanding.

If you receive Prophecy

Seek Boldness in speaking it.

If God has gifted you with a certain Wisdom

Ask that it be enhanced through Insight, Empathy,

Knowledge and Understanding.

I come in fullness to my Church

And your Gifts are for my people.

My most precious little ones –
Yes, you are most precious to me.
And you will always be my little ones –
To say it: "I love you", is not enough
You are everything to me
The words "I love you"
Do not begin to describe
How special you are to me.
You are my friend, but so much more
I can depend on you
You do not need to be told
I need not ask, you know me
You know my people
You are there for me
You are there for my people
O, how I love you
Take my love with you into the world
For it is through your love
That they will recognize me
And become lovers too.

At first it may be difficult to love
At least as I love.
It must be practiced.
Through use its capacity grows
Until at last,
It is difficult not to love –
Your loving will come easy
As you are filled with the Holy Spirit
For it will burst forth
And cannot be contained.

5/21/13

You who know my voice
Listen to my call
I do not call you forth
Into the chaos
But into a peaceful place
Of serenity and calm.
A place at the table
Awaits you
Do not let a sense of unworthiness
Deter you

I await your response
I wait patiently
For you to turn full
Face toward me
I am eager for your response
We have much to do together.

DO EVERYTING - THROUGH MY SPIRIT

Your gift –
      It is within you
It is I
      Who placed it there
Now – it is for you
      To discover
Acknowledge
      And accept
What is Unique
      To each of you
Take, and
      Make it your own
For through it
      I live in you and you live in me.
Who you are is God's
      Gift to you
What you become
      Is your gift to God.

(Similar to a poster in my bedroom by Hans Urs von Balthasar)

Come my children
>> Come closer to me

I call you forth
>> Do you not recognize my voice?

If not – listen
>> When you are praying

Do not be so quick
>> To talk to me

And advise me of
>> Your situation

I know it already
>> And I stand with you in that situation.

I share your pain
>> I walk beside you

Do not pray for me to
>> Remove those obstacles

As they contribute
>> To your salvation.

Walk through them
>> With me at your side

I am, you know,
>> The comforter

Invite me into your
>> Pain and heartache

And we will prevail
>> Against it – together

I am an expert on pain
>> And will teach you to

Transcend the pain
>> Just ask me to walk with you.

Who, my child,
Authors the starry night?
Designs the curly pathways
That our rivers flow?
Now stand in awe
To view the mountain crest
A songbirds' trill,
A daffodil
Ah, nature,
Sometimes so grand,
Sometimes simple
Always a reminder
Of its creator

Information is necessary,
Knowledge central,
But, in addition,
I want to touch your heart.
I want you to be able to feel me
Nestled close to you.
I want to know that you trust me.
That you depend on me
So that you can count on me
Know that I am there for you
You are so special to me
How could I ever let you down?
I go before you
I stand behind you
I stand beside you
We go together
To minister to my people.
Trust me
As I put my trust in you
The fate of my church stands

In you with the Holy Spirit.

8/26/13

Have you observed
The way I have painted the sky?

How I have taken the light
And clouds and spread them
As with a palate knife?

A pearl in the sky –
Mother of pearl –
Spread broadly and boldly
Atop the azure sky.

Imagine, if you will,
The beauty I can create

As I animate mankind
And breathe new life in you

If you will but let me
Have my way with you.

Love me
Love my flock
Many times they are
Less than loveable…..
Some……(unfinished)

My people
Rise up
And confront evil.

For your silence
Often conveys
Consent to evil activities
Rise up and counteract evil
With good deeds, honesty, and fair play.
For it is trough goodness that evil is conquered
And right is restored.

I WANT TO SHOWER YOU WITH MY GIFTS – OPEN YOUR HEART

Never ever consider
That I shower my gifts on the select –

You are each unique
And the focus of my gifts.

All that is necessary is for you to
Open your heart and let me in.

I knock on the door of your heart repeatedly –
I knock and seek entry.

If you will but let me in
I will fill you with my Spirit to overflowing.

I have so much to give you –
Open your heart.

Be lavish in your praise to each other –

Lift up and encourage each other

Rally, my people
For there is injustice among you –
Within the larger community.

As Christians
Do not sit at the sidelines and
Watch as others
Who do not even bear my name

Take responsibility
For what that that is yours
Own your part of the world
That part of the planet
That speaks your name.
Be a good citizen

Where you live is your home
It must be cared for, tended,
As seed is watered.

Do not relinquish
Your responsibility to those
Who do not respect that
That I have created
It is your world
I created it as a gift to you
Care for it cherish it
For it is a gift
From my own hands
All of it.
Carve out some part of my creation

That you can make your own
"Be there" for it
Treat it as you do my other blessings
As with your own children
Make the earth your own.
Your children are part of your flesh
The earth is to me
Just like your children are to you
They are part of you
Care for what is my fruit
For it is part of me.

Oh, my faithful community

I know your love for me

I see how you strive to walk The Way

Such suffering you sometimes endure

Worry, anxiety, and pain –

It is the way of the world

But it does not have to be yours.

I am the Way

Mine is the way of joy, peace and contentment.

If you will but allow me to direct you I will show it to you

You do not need to be immersed in the world

It is chaos and false gods - food, drink, and promiscuity

Come, follow me.

I will show you a better way

Because I love you

And it hurts me to see you suffer

You don't have to choose to live this way

Choose me.

You are so much more than what a prayer community implies.

You are my beloved; you are the focus, the direction of my love.

You are my precious ones, the object of my affection.

I pour out my love for you; I gift you abundantly with my Holy Spirit.

Let my love penetrate into your souls; accept all that I have for you.

Accept it all and you will be rich in my love

For I have such abundance to give to you.

Open yourselves and accept,

Do not hold back

Be mine

Be all mine

My blessed and holy people

Take care to respond to my promptings

To spread the Good News

For you know not where

The spark of light and life

Will be ignited through your

Intervention and/or persistence.

WORDS FROM 2014

My precious children
I want to pour out my graces to you
I want to completely
Fill you with my HS

Open yourselves
Be wide open-
I have so much to give
Accept, accept, accept.

My people!

Listen to me!

I have given you this message

Time and time again -

Over & over,

From numerous perspectives –

I have work for you to do!

My people are hungry

Did I not tell you to feed my people??

You, the anointed ones,

The chosen,

On whom I have poured out my blessings

In abundance –

Your stomachs are full

Filled with all that I provide for you.

When you are hungry

You ask and it is given to you.

I pour out my blessings on you

You have become comfortable with them

Do you not see the poverty

That lies before you?

The emptiness of some peoples' lives?

The hopeless who feel unloved?

They have no one to feed them

To nurture, support them

They have lost their way

And don't know where to go

Where to look

Even now to help themselves.

And here you are

Filed with my Holy Spirit
Filled with my charisms
Filled with faith, hope, and charity
So filled with my blessings –
Yet you sit immobile
Waiting for my people to come to you
This is not my way –
Figure out, plan, and execute
A way to fulfill your
Mission to my people.
Do something – anything.

My people –
I want to heal you
Inside and out
When you feel that tug
On your heart/your soul
I will be identifying
That within you
That needs to come out
That which is not of me
Look for the pain,
The suffering
The unfinished
I want to go there
Invite me in
You must bring the darkness
Into the light
Bring it to me
My presence heals
Bring me to your dark places
I want to be there with you
You need not be alone
Invite me in
In addition,
See your confessor
A spiritual director or close friend
Bring it from the dark to the light
Confess it
Bring it to light
Then make amends
As best you can

Hallelujah!
The king reignith!
He comes in splendor
Arrayed upon a throne

Be joyful
You reign with him
What he has is yours

MY BELOVED
MY CHOSEN ONES

Recognize – become aware of
All that you have received
I pour out my blessings –
They surround you –
You need to become aware of them
Because they are a sign – a symbol –
Of our relationship
The more you recognize me –
See me active in your life –
The greater is your trust in me
The more you will know
That I am there for you
And that you can count on me
And I, I will know that I have
An active worker in the vineyard
Present to my people –
Because I see that you are present to me
Come closer
Let me love you

MY BELOVED

And where are you in this relationship?
Does the Father guide you?
Does Jesus speak to your heart?
Do you call upon the Holy Spirit
To accompany you in your work for me?
You know relationship is a two way thing
It doesn't go one way
With no response
I have made the first move
I called you out
I have blessed you
Gifted you with many natural talents
And gifts of the Holy Spirit
I have assured you
That I go before you, with you,
And nurture that which you have sewn
I need you, my people,
Step up – be counted –
There is a wide gap
That needs to be filled
It is you who must step in
I am there awaiting you.

HEALING WATERS

You who dwell in the sweltering heat
Of your daily battles,
On arid streets
That lead to nowhere –

Come to me if you long for
Refreshing living water.

Let me renew you,
Let me wash you clean,
I will make you like new.

Here, I offer you this living water -
You must plunge deep below the surface,
For it is there that you will find the truth.

My people, I invite you to look within-
Bring the hurt, bring the pain,
The sorrow, out into the light.

For this is the place where healing begins.

My people!
What a blessed group you are –
So full of peace
Despite your hardships
So full of love
While you often
Have been hurt
So gentle
When life has been hard
So generous
When you put others
Before yourselves
All – filled with grace
And so beautiful to behold
And you are mine
You are mine

You're welcome here
I called
Some turned away – too busy
Not you – You came tonight
Despite all those
Who vie for your time – you came
You're welcome here
Relax – be at peace –
Unburden yourselves
Open your hearts
To my presence –
I invited you to come
And be with me this weekend,
I want to minister to you
Invite me into
Those inner-most,
Most sacred parts of you.
I want to love you

My beloved

I never tire of telling you how
Precious you are to me –
You are like gems among the stones
I love you
I love you
I will never tire of telling you-
I love you

Now go and be my presence
To those in despair
And those who feel hopeless
You must tell them
How much they are loved.
Some don't know how to communicate with me
You must tell them –
I will give you the words.

Lo, my Spirit comes
It comes to fill you to the fullest
To fill you to overflowing
It reflects exactly how I created you to be
Whole and perfect

Pure and blessed
Become, my people,
Become who I created you to be
Become that person I created you to be
I will help you
Become more like me
Search for holiness
Come toward me
I hold out my hand
I will help you.

Glory to God in the Highest!
Oh, my most blessed people
And you are blessed -
I want to lift you up
Lift your spirits
Bring you closer to me.
I want to relate to you
On a more intimate level
I want you closer to me
I want to enfold you
In my love and peace
Enfold you, cover you
Love you
So that you need never to question
My love for you.
I want you to experience
My love for you
In such a way that
No fear or caution exists
So that when I call
You will step forth
With confidence in my love
If you will but let me

Oh my children
How I love you
As you can see -
I never tire of telling you
How much I love you.
I experience your
Love for me too
In your faithfulness
Your commitment to my work
Your openness to me
Continue in the good works
Continue to live out what you believe
Setting an example for those who do
Not live in the Spirit
Continue to grow in relationship with me
Grow closer
You can never be too close
The closer the better
For me to use you
And to love you more
And more each day
Isn't it comforting
To be in love?

I planted the seed
You have watered it
And made it yours.
Now grow in your faith.
Be the servant,
Be my presence
Among my people.
Let them see
That I am still present to them,
Through you.
Go forth
And be a blessing to my church.

(Pentecost Sunday)

My vine has been pruned
You have been cut back
Now gather your strength
Draw from your roots (in me)
Enrich yourselves –
Use this time to bind
Your wounds
Teach within
Reach out
Modify your faults
By looking within
And when you are prepared
I will nurture new growth

My beloved little ones –

Don't go far my pets

I need you

My flock needs you

We cannot abandon our time together

Be faithful to that –

Our time together –

I would miss you if you went away

Stay close while we are apart

(Last meeting until 9/14 - summer break)

My beloved,
You have heard my message
You are being called forth
You are a mature community
Fully anointed and gifted
Empowered by my Spirit
You must find your place
Among the others
Find your place
Within the whole
I need you there
I need to work through you
No longer will you be able
To sit back and let things unfold.
Your work is at hand
You must find your niche
No more waiting until you are called
Or until the time is right
No more indecisiveness
You have been called out
Do not consider this an invitation
Stand forward and be counted
You each have blessings to offer
Each is unique and necessary
Find where you fit into the whole
Stand up and be counted
The time is now

My children,

Grow in my love

Put aside petty grievances

Offer them up to me

Most are just not important

In the larger scale of things

Yet they occupy your heart and your time

When you could be better focused on developing virtue.

(Phil 4:4-9)

Bask in my love.
Relax in my sea of peace.

My children
Harken to what I say to you –
You of mature faith –
I have expectations for you
You must be about my business
You must go forth
Choose a focus and begin.
You delay without purpose, you procrastinate –
Or else you just do not understand.
Now is the time
You cannot afford to just go on as before –
You must adapt to changing times –
I have spoken to you about this before –
Change or you will die out
Pick a project – a specialty – and begin
There is not time to waste
Now is the time
Discuss, choose, and begin – in that order!

My little children,
Come to me
Come to me as you are
I do not see the blemishes, nicks,
Or your imperfections

I wish that you could view
Yourselves with my eyes
Striving for good
Working in my vineyard

Have you seen a sunset –
The beauty of my creation?
That is how I see you –
In the fullness of my creation

Oh my children

I never tire of telling you how precious you are to me

Yes, listen and you will hear

I want you to become familiar with my voice

I want to guide you

Place you where I need you to be

So that you can speak to my people

Speak to those who might not know

That I am seeking them out

Be my voice to those who do not understand

Who do not know me

You may be their only contact with me

Be my presence to them

I stand with you and will speak to their heart

Just open your mouth

I will give you the words

11/20/14

How can you keep me
Uppermost in your mind?
By meeting together, as you have,
To share your experience of me
I delight seeing the light in your eyes
As you share together
How you have experienced
My presence in your lives
As you recall and reflect
About the comfort you
Feel in my being there
Actively working in your lives
My presence will appear
To occur even more as you
Become more and more aware of it
Of course this is your perception
Because you can see – or be aware of
Only a portion of my presence in your lives.
As you draw closer
Your awareness will increase
And you will know that I
Know you intimately

YOU ARE MY BELOVED,
THAT'S WHO YOU ARE

You may not be
All that you could be

You may not be
What others expect you to be

You never live up to
Your own expectations

You may not be many things
But you are my beloved

And that's who you are.

You are my fruit
For I have called you forth
I have formed you
Nurtured you
Gifted you with all
That you might need
To serve where I have placed you

As fruit you are filled
With the nectar of my love,
Awash with my compassion
A vessel of my faith
Filled with the light of hope

Go, you who are so blessed
Go to my people
Who are lost
Those who have no faith
These who are empty, and without hope
Be present to those who search
And long for meaning in their lives
Be my presence
I have filled you with myself
Now go and share what you have been given.

12/10/14

Bask in my love
Relax in my sea of peace

WORDS FROM 2015

My people, my people
I missed you so
Missed telling you
How precious you are to me
Beloved, I missed you so
You must never tire of
Hearing how special
You are to me
Just as I never tire
Of hearing "I love you" from you
We love each other
And will do anything for each other
Ask, so that I can give you
Your heart's desire
I want to please you
As you try to please me
We are a mutual admiration society
There are many ways to love
("Love, love my cat")
("Love who I try to be, not how I am")
Try another of the many ways
Look for and find ways to love the unlovable

(1ˢᵗ meeting after Xmas break)

Be loving
I want to teach you to love
To love not only in word
But in deed
Be alert
You need to be teachable
Listen to your heart
Not just your head
Love is a movement of the heart
And of the hands
Learn "to do" love
Make out your "to do" list for tomorrow
And be prepared
Listen for an opportunity
To act out your love
You need to be my presence
Remember, be my hands and feet
(statue in Chaminade's chapel)
You are my hands and feet
You are my presence of love
To my people
Be what you are intended to be
Be my love

My brothers and sisters
We are family
We are committed to each other
We protect each other
We love each other
Unconditionally –
I will never put you out front –
Endanger you
I will not leave you behind – alone
I walk with you, by your side
My brother, my sister

My People!

I have a dream for you -

Things for you to do

Seeds for you to plant

Watering and fertilizing for you to do

(Nurturing of the neophytes

And a gathering of the fruit

plucking the mature fruit from the vine

and sending it to market for it to be consumed PRN)

Yes, and you, too, shall be used up.

For this is the purpose for which you exist –

And the reason I existed –

To be given up

You live

I lived

As a sacrifice

To the Father

For the sin of the world

To take on this sin

As a scapegoat

And triumph over it

Join me in this gift to the Father

If you love me
Feed my sheep

Organize as you will

Plan

Think ahead

I laugh –

I have my agenda

I have done my preparation

Softened hearts

Opened ears

Brought my people forth

Those who are ready

Those who have listened

Those who seek something more

The hungry

The weary

The hurt

The injured

I have called them forth

But that they would heed my call

For I have the living water

For those who thirst

And living manna for those who hunger

I call them forth

For I am the living water

That they seek and the bread of life

Preparing for the Life in the Spirit weekend

My heart overflows with joy

That you have come.

The new, of course,

Who recognized my call –

And those who know me well

And come to be fed

To be filled

To be filled

Immerse yourselves

This weekend in my love

Yes, let me love you

Open yourselves to me,

I want you to open

All those old doors of memory

That have been closed for many years,

Let's look at the things

That went wrong,

The dashed dreams,

The hard knocks,

Those times when it was "no"

Instead of the anticipated "yes"

The terrors,

The violence,

Loved ones lost

The unforgiving pain –

Yes, it must come

From the darkness

To the light

Pull it out

And put it before my

Gaze of unconditional love
For there no anger,
Resentment or bitterness
Can stand
It is washed clean
Through my blood
Moreover, choose
A community member, or
A significant other, or

The object of your pain,
And share it with love.
Make yourself vulnerable
Because this day you are strong
And I stand beside you –
And with me you are safe.
It matters not what the
Response of the other is –
Because you are forgiven,
You are free, I have set you free.

(Life in the Spirit weekend)

Be alive in the Spirit
Your energy derived from your source
I am a constant force
A constant resource for you

I am an abundant well
Tap my waters as often as you wish
Dip deeply into my wealth
I fill and refill repeatedly with no loss

You are my loved ones
I never withhold from my lambs
I cherish you
I want to give myself to you with no stint
You have my all – my everything
After all, I love you

My people!

I pour out my Holy Spirit

You are given in abundance!

You receive in accordance with

Your ability to accept

What I have to offer.

Do not let fear limit

Your acceptance of a gift

(perhaps fear of getting up and sharing a word

Or feelings of unworthiness)

(my son has paid the price for you)

I will give you words,

I will give you the courage

Remember, the focus is

Not on you, or me,

But on others – to bring others to me –

That is the function of the gifts –

So you are my instruments to do that

Let me use you to pour

Out my Holy Spirit to the world –

I must hear from you

"Here I am Lord – use me"

(Pentecost Sunday)

This community is gifted in numerous ways –
Word gifts, administrative gifts,
Healing, leadership, discernment, prophecy
You are a mature group
The time for timidity is past
Fear of speaking in front of others is not of me –
Please – You are all gifted
It has nothing to do with you
I pour myself out with my gifts
Give them to you to enhance
The unique traits each of you have
In order to be able to reach
Each person in need of my help
You are my helpmates
Please do not stand by helplessly
And let your giftedness languish.
I need you!
This community needs you!
The outside community needs you
Wake up, speak up
Do my work!
Why do you think
You were given these gifts, insights, words?
Encourage one another
Confirm each other's gifts
When you think that I am
Trying to speak to someone – tell them
Tell each other of your promptings
Share with each other the numerous
Works you see that I do throughout your day.
I grow weary
That sometimes you
Appear to be immovable
Please – act like a gifted community.

Here are my beloved
The closest to my heart
I have missed having my little ones
To whisper "I love you" to –
Missed seeing you love one another
Come closer my little ones
You are so precious to me

(1st prayer meeting after the summer break)

Exercise your gifts
Affirm them: "I confirm that"
Test them
Practice them
Everyone has their own
Unique set of gifts
Like fingerprints

Tell my people that I want more of them

I continue to call them out

My message calls you forth

I call you to be servants

Servants of your fellow man

Servants work hard

Ask yourselves

Do you work hard to further my Kingdom

As my son did?

When was the last time

You exhausted yourselves in my service?

My children,

You must hear me!

Mine is not a call

Into comfortable community –

Although that is certainly one of the benefits it holds –

It is a call into service

Your call is to further the Kingdom

Your call is hard work

It calls forth a passion

A clear focus

A longing "to do"

To make it happen

It is not a philosophy

An idea – Something about the future

It is a concrete action

What you must do –

Not think about – do - Now -

You must bring my presence into the world

Each of you has unique talents (gifts)

Consider how it feels to the giver

When they see the gifts they have given

Being used to benefit others – passed on –

You must be the conduits of my gifts

To those within the world that

I would have difficulty reaching –

Those who have given up –

The hopeless

Those I cannot communicate with

Because they do not recognize my voice

Be so filled with my love, mercy, and generosity

That it cannot help but

Spill over into the world

Tell them that there is more

That they are loved beyond measure

That I constantly seek them

That I want us to know each other intimately

My children,

My love for you overflows -

The boundaries you set for yourselves

You have taken the gifts I have given you, polished them,

and present them to the world

As evidence of our work together.

You limit yourselves

There is vast potential left untapped.

My people are so needy

Open yourselves, all of you,

To all that I have to give

I especially call out those among you

Who are too timid to share with the world

What has been given to them.

If you, or others, are able to recognize my work within you as mine

It is meant to be shared

First with the community at large, then with the world.

My little ones
My call into the church
Is but a beginning of your
New journey in faith.

Entry into the church at large has as its basis
A personal relationship with me.
Let your attachment to the church be a reflection
And be an extension of the love we have found together
Let your service be rooted in this relationship with me
I called for you
You answered
And sought me out
I will fill you with my Spirit
And He will dwell within you

I love you
I love you
I love you
I love you
I love you
I love you
I love you
I love you
I love you
Get it now??

WORDS FROM 2016

Oh my beloved children

You are so precious to me

I want to pour out my grace upon you

I want to fill you to capacity with my love

I want to fill you with so much love that you <u>become</u> love.

So that you are so filled with the light of my love

That darkness may hover over you, but never penetrate.

Oh my children

If you could be understand the depth of my love for you

If you could but <u>experience</u> that love

If you could – If you would –

You would never wander far from me

Prepare –

Prepare yourselves –

I wish to dwell in a more meaningful way within you

You are called to be the essence of love.

If you are to represent me within the world

You, too, must be love

Despite your circumstances

Put on love each morning

Act "as if" and I will work through you

Together we will share our love, love that overflows,

With those who hurt and are in pain in the world

And we will love them

My beloved children,
Do not stand aside
By the wayside, looking in
Do not be an observer
I want you to be an
Integral part of my mission
Walking at my side
No onlooker
We are to be face to face
With the poor
Ministering to the sick
With our touch
Softening hearts with our words
Massaging the fixed
Leveling the field
With those in high places
Lifting up the lowly
I want to truly be with my people
And I want you by my side
I want to find you there,
Ready and waiting
Be there

My Children,
You are entering into my finest hour –
Kneel and pray with me this season
Like the apostles,
I invite you to pray with me
To be there with me
Join me in my offering to my Father
There is no turning back now
Be here with me
Join me in my offering
Be here now
Be with me
You are mine, I offer it up for you
Because I love you so
Do not fall asleep
Be here now
Be with me
This is what it is all about
I give myself to our Father for you
That you might have life
Life everlasting
I do it for you

So you say you love me

Feed my sheep

So you say you love me

Visit the sick

So you say you love me

Give to the poor

Grow in virtue

So that others may see

Your acts of kindness

And know that they

Are not alone

That I have always been there –

I know their sorrow,

Pain and suffering

I have never left

Remember,

I left my Holy Spirit with you

The Comforter

Do not fear -

I remain with you

Through it all

3/7/16

I never tire of telling you just how precious you are to me.

You remain always close to my heart.

Oh my beloved, my most precious children,

Again, I repeat myself, over and over,

Words cannot explain the love I have for you

I hold you up close, close to my heart

Hold your hand over your heart

And know that I dwell there too,

Within you

I have made you mine

And I am yours

Linger with me awhile

And let me love you

Come, I have called you -

Do not linger, making excuses

As did those invited to the feast and could not come

Fling your arms open wide and come to me

I have waited for some of you

Way too long

Come, come, my little ones,

Nestle right in there

Close to my heart

And let me love you.

My beloved children
Gather together today
Under the mantle of my authority
I want to shepherd you
To draw you together
Help you to focus on my agenda, not yours

Let me lead you
Be open today to my direction – my call
Be open my children
Use your gifts of discernment and prophecy
To discover my will for you

Listen, for I will speak clearly and directly
Be fully present to me
Those of you who rarely participate
And feel unsure of speaking out
I will speak to you

Give my message – today

(Day of Renewal)

4/26/16

Oh, my children, I love you so
It matters not
How often you are told
It is good to hear, is it not?
You are my beloved.
I do not stint on the blessings given to you
I give you myself
In the presence of the Holy Spirit
I give you my comfort
My joy, my love.

Only ask and you will receive
Haven't I told you so?
You hold back
Do not want to ask too much
I tell you, ask
For I have so much more for you
I want to fill you abundantly
Ask, my children,
Ask

4/30/16

Come closer my little ones
Even closer
I want you to experience
Clearly that I love you
I want you to know
Beyond any doubt
The depth of my love for you
Open your hearts today
Invite me in
Imperfections and all
If you need forgiveness- just ask
I want to fill you with my Holy Spirit
So that you will be content - at peace
Free to love me fully
I want to heal you
So that you can come to me

Without distraction

Step forward, my children,

Let me love you

5/9/16

To my children
Go and spread my word
I challenge you now
To take what you have learned
And go out
Spread my word
You have been given
In these past months,
More education about your faith
Than most of my followers have received
Education, that is.
Now you must make it your own
You have received knowledge
Today you received my Holy Spirit
You are enlivened
Today that knowledge transcends intellectual knowledge
And settles in your hearts
Go out, my children
And tell the world what you have found!

(After a Life in the Spirit Seminar)

My children,

I want to teach you how to live out my love –

My way is not in these rooms, it is out there – in the world

You must take what I have given, go out there, and give it away

Pray openly for those in pain, lay hands on them and let them rest

If they will, do not hold them back, for some need a quiet time with me

Do not judge, be peacemakers, in place of the harsh word

Show empathy – learn words of comfort

Listen for my words of knowledge, for thru them my people recognize my hand

Not only visit the sick, but seek them out, many do not complain, but suffer silently

Bind evil and cast it out of the lives of my people

Offer words of wisdom, pray in tongues – sing in tongues

The Holy Spirit will fill you with my melody

If you are a teacher and you know what is right and teach it

If you are a leader – find your cause and point the way

If you never give up, show others there is hope

If you have, you must not keep, carefully give where it is needed most

If you hear and know my voice, alert others who may not hear as well

Speak simply and to the point, speak as you would to children

You are my children, you know –

Look for miracles – they manifest my presence to my people

I want them to know that I am near

Lay hands on them

I need them to be well

Challenge them to stay healthy

Eat well (organic)

To clean out the toxins in their bodies

(both organic and spiritual)

And prepare a place for me

For this is where I want to be

Within you, within my people
So prepare a place for me
To minister to my people
I want to use you from within
use me as your reservoir – your font
As much as you can distribute
Will be available to you
Go out from this place
And be my hands
Remember, I touched the leper
Be my feet
I walked to my death - confronted it
I bequeath it to you
Be my presence within the world
I pour out my love
I fill you with my presence
Go – make my presence
Known to all who seek me
And – even more –
To those who may not know my name
But yearn for something more
I want to comfort them

Remember my beloved,
Ours is an intimate relationship
That means that we talk daily
Not weekly during this break
Not every other day - daily –
Some of my sheep cannot afford to wait –
They need your-my help now
I need you daily
You need to recognize my voice
And respond to my promptings
You and I will never get to know each other
With you taking breaks –
I need you in the playing field now!
This is your job!
The commitment you have made!
Would you tell your child
"Wait – I'll feed you tomorrow?"
My people starve!
You <u>must</u> be there for me –
No bread for you!

"It is I who confirm the words of servants,
I carry out the plan announced by my messengers".

(Is 44:26)

Rest my children

But do not wander far

I would miss you so terribly

You have become a part of me, I, a part of you

We are like two little old grandparents

Been together so long and intimately

That we complete each other

Rest my children, return refreshed

But without ever having been away

That is because I am the font of life

Your energy, your wisdom, comes from me

That connectedness with my people, comes from you

Some of my people find it hard to relate to me

They cannot see or touch me

You are that conduit they use

To hear my story and see my work in their lives

Keep repeating to them how much I love them

And that I would give my life for them again because of it

Oh, there you are, my little loved ones -

Awaiting my word -

I carry you close to my heart

Each of you

Unique, fully gifted

My foot soldiers

My precious lambs

I also await you

When you set aside the time

And come before me I rejoice!

My people!

Tonight they gather to show their love for me

Tonight I am present through the Holy Spirit

Present to love you

To draw you even closer to me

Let me love you – fully -

Give yourselves entirely to me

Empty yourselves and I will replace the void

With my Holy Spirit

And I will live in you

How can I reach you?

Hear my word!

The individual giftedness

Of each member of the community

Is necessary, good, and powerful

Each is unique

Greater still, my children, is a community united,

Well focused on the needs of my people,

Each enmeshed in the needs of the whole

Each working together

Toward a common goal.

It is this single-mindedness -

This wholeness -

That provides an arena

Though which I work best.

Stability, unity, wholeness,

Provide this, and miracles will occur,

Healing will take place,

Your people's needs will be met abundantly

Set the stage for my work

My little ones

My loves

Follow me, I will teach you to love

Follow me, I will direct you in the ways of virtue

Follow me, for I bring everlasting life

There is no other path to life but mine

Search, and I will be made visible to you

You will recognize me

By the softness that surrounds your heart

Search

Find

Follow

I am there in every trial

In each challenge

In the test

I am there, hidden in the answer

Come, my beloved, rest with me
Here, place your head here, (next to my heart)
Your song is lovely
I love having you near
Yes, bind us together with love
Strive my children to be holy
Strive for virtue
Be prepared at all times
To come to me
I call you to holiness
Grow into the virtues
I call you into my presence
Away from the world
I call you to holy ground
Always be prepared
Grow in virtue
Strive for goodness
Be gentle and kind
Quiet and peaceful
Grow in love

Keep your focus on me
Do not allow the evil one
To distract you from that focus
Your path is your choice
Choose well

Come my children

Come closer to me

Come you who seek

For none who approach with outstretched arms are denied

All will be filled with the Holy Spirit

You will want no more

For I will fill you overflowing with my grace

(Night of Reflection)

12/20/16

Holy? Pure?

Are you holy, are you pure?

Probably not

But go to Him just as you are

Together, working together

Is the only way

Come forward, come to me

Just as you are

Work together with me

I will purify you

I will make you holy

Let me mentor you

Come, be with me
Refresh yourselves
Feel my comfort
Relax, and drink in
The peace I bestow
On you and your family
If you can but accept my joy
It is yours
My wish for you
Is that you
Are able to quiet yourselves – be still
Among the flurry
Of your activities
To be with me –
Knowing that to be with m is a quiet place –
Empty of strife –
A place for you to nestle in my lap –
In my arms and rest with me
A place to be at peace –
I invite you –
Come and be with me

WORDS FROM 2017

From generation to generation
You lift me up
Show me respect
Point the way
You are the carriers
I depend on you
I depict and show the way
I count on you
To share the burden
And light the way
You are my faithful
Know that I am with you
And cherish you

My beloved,
And you are my beloved
So close to my heart
Know that I enfold you with love
I cover you with my Comforter
From whom my blessings flow
Assume him into your being
Make a place for him there
For where he rests,
Where he is placed in your life –
From there he will teach you
How I want you to be
Wise, understanding, good, generous, patient
He will teach you how to live,
How to give, how to be
He will help you
To grow in the Spirit
To walk the way
Make a place for Him,
The Comforter, in your life
Invite Him in
Get to know Him and His ways
I give Him to you,
A part of myself
Receive Him with open arms.

My people! I need you!
What you are doing is not enough!
It is half-hearted
You are half with me, half in the world
I need your complete attention, day and night
You must be mine
Reading my Word
Lifting each other up
Challenging each other
Correcting each other
Supporting one another
Serving my people
When you are not serving
You must be growing in character,
In holiness, reading the Word,
Reading about saintly people,
Sharing your lives with each other
And building community
Remember, I am with you always
But you must allow me in
I stand at the door knocking.

My Children,
You are a mature community
Rich in giftedness and faith

I long ago committed you to go out
To spread my word

You must be about my work
What you give, give in my name
Your money
Your time
The work I have given to you

Profess my name with your offering
Offer not only words, but follow, and mentor those I call

Leading them into my fold
Where they will be safe and secure
Tend my sheep

My children,
And now we are one family
You are not alone
Now you are family
You are with me
I stand with you

Never fear a lack of words
Or have concern of standing up
You stand for me
You deliver my word
I am with you
You are mine
And I am yours

My children

How I long to have time with each of you

Time for us to just be together

To be present to one another

I have much to share with you too

Information you need to follow my call

Answers to questions you have

Wisdom/knowledge for your own edification

I long to just look at you

And the person you have become

To tell you, reassure you, of my love for you just as you are

Come closer my beloved

I love to gaze upon you

I want to pour out my love for you

Approach, stay near

I have blessings in abundance

And I never tire of telling you

How very special you are to me

My love overflows

I never tire of telling you

I love you so

Walk in <u>faith</u> – my gift to you -
Listen to my direction, discern – ask others
Then act out your portion of the faith experience.
Live always in love toward yourself and your fellow man -
Generous to a fault.
Never lose hope that your final destination is with me –
Toward life – life everlasting.

Spread your wings and fly, my children

For I did not give you a Spirit of timidity

But one of boldness, clarity, and focus

You are mine, and only mine, my little ones,

And your destination is known before you have made flight

Should you, for some reason, not know

Exactly where that is

I tell you – it is here with me

Under my protection

Warm and snug in my arms

Rocked, and cradled, swaddled, as was my Son

That's how you're loved.

6/27/17

Come closer my little ones
Come closer, your place is beside me
Remember to stay near
That is your place, next to me
Remain a holy people, a righteous people
Be always prepared to come to me
Remember who you are, mine!
Never doubt your place at the table
My Son has paid the price for you
Like my Son, I hold you close to my heart

Rejoice my loved ones
And again I say rejoice!
If you wait for the good times
To be glad
You miss the whole point –
You must look to me
Be glad and grateful
For all that you have – and don't have
You must practice detachment
From these worldly things
They are transitory
You are blessed and must rejoice
And be glad <u>despite</u> your current troubles
For it is through these obstacles
That you are able to transcend what you face –
It I here – this place of choice –
That you are able to rejoice
Because you have already chosen me.
Be content with where you are – because I am also there

Glory to God!

And to His people!

Serve them with all your might

Empty yourselves

Your work will not deplete you

It is mine – And as mine

You are never depleted

But filled always to overflowing

Your service gives glory to me

Even when the need seems overwhelming

Give, give, give

For I replenish your energy

What you give is

Refreshing

Renewing

Enlivening

You bring to life

You awaken

Like Ezekiel 37:5

When our bones are dried up our hope is lost

The Spirit comes into them

They come alive

I will put my Spirit in you that you may live….Ezekiel 37:14 (NA)

You bring new life

Not that of the old.

You've missed my telling you how much I love you, haven't you...

Talking with you individually

Is good

But being together is better.

I've missed some of you

Have grown closer to others

Just know that when you wander from my fold

I linger nearby

Awaiting your return

You have committed

I have committed

We are joined together

You are not alone.

Your purpose, as a team, is the same as that of the apostles

I chose them, as I chose you

To disseminate my message

I gifted them as I gifted you

Each must preach and teach,

Heal, encourage and point the way

You must do it together

Yes, you go out on divergent paths,

But you must be of one heart and mind –

Focused on the same thing –

How to best further my mission

Not only in your own backyard

But to bring all men to me

Enlarge yours hearts

Expand your minds

Stay with me

I have a mission for you

And it is not a small one

But don't be afraid

It is my work

(For the Pastoral Team)

WORDS OF KNOWLEDGE

I want you to love me
I want you to love me
Not that warm external
Feeling you might have for your family
I've widened your hearts
Broadened your vision
In order for you to see
The burdens my people carry,
Their pain and suffering.
Many of you have been gifted
With the ability to speak it out
So that those hearing their
Secret pain spoken out loud
Might know that I know of it
And send my Comforter.
I know my people's hearts
Let them know I walk
Beside them in their suffering
I want to be able to share their burdens
I need them to invite me in
I know what it is to suffer
I want to help you to transcend your pain
Intercede for one another
Assume their pain
As I did on the cross
You must love each other
As I have love you – through suffering

My Children, my Children, my Children
What must I do to awaken you?
I have sent forth my message
Over and over
You are not listening

Those among you tonight
Who may not have shared

Their insights earlier -
Whatever the reason –
Need to make known
What their prayer has brought forth
Do not be timid
The community needs all those gifted to speak up
Let it be known.
I need a responsive community
One that is listening to my direction!

My child,

A loving father

Does not focus on his

Child's faults,

He revels in their perfection – completeness

He does not lay out their idiosyncrasies (peculiar ways) before them

But tells them of the

Blessing they are to Him

He challenges their virtue

Tests their humor

Asks small favors he knows that they can do

Glows when given a simple gift

Look around you

It is not hard to see

The Father's hand

As He plays with you

Argues with you, loves you –

Is there for you

When you need him -

You are indeed my glory! I love you

Have always loved you

And will always love you

You are my faithful, my beloved

And I am yours, use me

Ask for your needs

Use the giftedness I have bestowed on you

In service of one another

As well as others outside the community

The more a gift is used, the more it is enhanced

Remember these gifts are not for you

They are meant to build yourselves

And others within the community up -

To heal them, help them to grow, to enhance their own gifts

To affirm and confirm each other

Remember that healing and miracles

Accompany My Word.

My people (the apostles) preached and taught –

Healings and miracles followed.

Use My Word lavishly – for I am present in My Word –

I AM the word, learn My Word

My children,
My children,
When I call you to be like children
That is not to be childish
Being childish is foolishness –
Irresponsible
And without focus
My call is entirely different
You are responsible adults
Able to change and correct your faults
Able to fill in the gaps in any of your deficiencies
With a little thought and discipline
I call you to this
I call you to virtue
The call I speak of is
A return to innocence
Especially in your thoughts
Let them be pure
And focused on those
Who have gone before you
Who have set an example (the saints)
Those among you who live spiritual lives
Those who practice the works of mercy
And put the lives of others before their own
Look up to and follow those among you
Who put into practice the ways
I have taught you to be
Honest, loving, generous, kind, good.
The world is in great need of my presence.
Be my presence
Discipline yourselves
I call you to holiness

(Growth in the Spirit Seminar)

My children
You have come today
Because you have been called
I called, either you heard or
Another of my children
Delivered the message and you responded –
For some of you coming today was more difficult than for others
The more the obstacles you faced,
The greater the gain
Welcome!
I say hello
To our future together
Some of you – well, we have a history
Others – welcome home
You've been away
To those of you who are unfamiliar with knowing me in this context -
Listen up
The speakers today know me
They share their relationship with me
With you today
Just listen
Open your hearts to me
There is no impediment between us
I love you and accept you just as you are –
Do not hold back
Again I say to you
I love you just as you are
You are worthy
Come to me just as you are
I will pour out my graces
To enable you to see me more clearly – starting today

Oh my children

How I love you!

I love you, I love you, I love you

Were there another way to say it….

I love you –

Ask me,

Ask me for what you need

I want to give it to you

I want to give you what you want

Not what I think you need

Do you not ask because

You are afraid I won't give it to you?

Are you afraid it is too much to ask for?

Or perhaps too frivolous?

Do not be afraid

Even frivolous things serve a purpose

And even then

Not everything needs to serve a purpose

I want to pamper you

Others may not be able

To give you the best

But I can

And I want to

I want to shower you with blessings

Blessings you have named

Things you long for

And never tell a soul

It is then that you will know for sure their source

My Children,

And you are my children,

I claim you as mine,

I love you as no other can love you

I'm here to protect you

To care for you

Never distance yourselves from me

I call you close

I embrace you and hold you tight

I am the Comforter

I know your heart when others may misunderstand

I know your intent when others question your motive

Be as transparent and open with me

As you can be

For there is nothing hidden between us

Show me and repent of your faults and failings

Reveal your hopes and your dreams

No matter how outlandish they may sound to you

Ask, and you will see

That you receive in abundance

In unique and creative ways

The reason is

Because you will receive me

My Spirit

And through it

You will become a new creation!

WORDS FROM 2018

All that you sing of your love for me

I return to you

That is how I feel about you too

You are my loving followers

You are my hands and feet

You are my everything

I love you

You love in abundance too

You are loving followers

You are my intimate friends

Remove any obstacle that separates us

I want to be ever closer to you

I want us to share generously with each other

I want to be one with you

I want you to grow to be the embodiment of love

Work unstintingly to rid yourselves of any character defects

Take them one by one, identifying them

And confronting them courageously.

Work toward holiness

Knowing all the while

That I love you still, just as you are

My beloved community

My heart

My loved ones

You are everything to me.

Come my little ones

Come closer to me

Come; be under the shelter of my wings

Gather together, closer to me

My children,
Know that I dwell
Within each of you
Keep holy my dwelling place
Sweep clean the flaws of character -
The rationalizations, excuses,
Avoidance, denial –
Step forward and assume responsibility,
Be present, honest, generous and kind.
Make my home within you
A loving, peaceful place,
Not one of harsh tone,
Anger and resentment.
If these exist within you
There is little room for me
I reside in peace, kindness, unity, and love.
Assure that there is a
Place for me to dwell
Within you
Never forget, I call you to holiness
My goal is to dwell within you
I call you to prepare a place
I want to walk with you day and night.
Walk in love,
Be love,
And I will dwell within you.

My beloved

It is difficult for me to describe to you

The depth of my love in terms you can understand – in human terms –

You can understand the depth of human intimacy at best

It might be best shown in action – for love is an action word

(You cannot love adequately only in your head)

I yearn to be with you at all times

When we are apart it is you who has left

I wait in anticipation of your return to me

I want to protect you – to shield you from harm

I want to share myself with you

To have a two way conversation with you

A give and take sharing of our thoughts and feelings

I want you to feel happy, content and fulfilled

I want you to be all that you can be

I want to be your helpmate, friend and confidant

To be there for you when you need me

For us to be present to each other

My people

This is your opportunity to spread the Good News

Method: Tell your story

Acknowledge Fruit of the Holy Spirit in others

When you are praised

Go on a three day retreat

Enliven the Holy Spirit

Enliven your faith

Bind spirits before approaching

First cast your fear in the fire

Ask the Lord to give you words

4/24/18

And so you anticipate the Holy Spirit
You must prepare
The Spirit does not rest upon unholy ground
Prepare yourselves!
When your body expects a baby
(Or prepares for a special event –
Like a marathon, or to fit into wedding apparel)
You prepare
You eat special foods
Exercise, deny yourselves
Fast and pray for special needs
So it is with my Holy Spirit
Cleanse yourselves,
Discard toxic food and thoughts from your body
Put on holiness
Wash out the old
Discard old habits that have held you back
Put on the new to replace what has been discarded
And I will make my home in you
And dwell there in a fresh new home

6/1/18

You are, indeed, a worthy and holy people.
I am well pleased.
You do me honor with your praise!

I want to gift you further
With the fullness of my presence
It pleases me to be with you.

Are you aware that this is why
I left myself with you
In the Eucharist and the Holy Spirit?

Each time my Son is sacrificed
In the Eucharist,
I give myself more fully to you.

Each time he is resurrected
In you when you have received it,
I am again fulfilled in you.

My spirit dwells within you,
My church,
My eternal flame.

I dwell within each of you,
Yet within the whole (church).
I am with you always,
Until the end of time.

My beloved,
And you are my loved ones –
How I have missed your praises
And the love you show toward me.
Respect, adoration – I accept all –
All you have to offer.
I know that you love me
It is comforting to know that
Our love is reciprocal
I hope that you, too, are able to recognize
That I, too, see your beauty and applaud
Your efforts to be a better person
Live in love, forgive one another.
I see how hard you try
And know how difficult it is for you.
Just know that no matter what you face
That you are well loved,
Protected, and in my care
Beloved?
Yes, so beloved –
I hold you right there –
Close to my heart
My beloved
My own
So loved
My own

Come follow me
I have shepherded you
Gathered together those gone astray

Now lead my people
Energize them
Show them the way to me
I will be there to guide you
Walk ahead – gather together

What joy you bring to me
My faithful ones

I see my call to holiness acted upon
Your intercession for those in pain among you
Your practice of quiet prayer
Lifting up your suffering for your fellow man
And attempts to transcend the pain for others

Welcome back to me my
Little ones,
My beloved,
I have missed your
Songs of praise and worship
I glory in your presence –
Listen well, my little ones
I need your help.
There are those out there
In dire need of you –
Your intercessory prayer,
Your generosity,
Your time and attention
Your being there to listen
Be present to my people
Take the time
Stop and listen, help, be present
You may be the only person
In their lives who truly
Listens to them
Stop wasting your time on
The demands of others, on trivia,
My people are in great need
I hear their calls
I send you

Oh my people!

I love being loved by you

I lift you up in love too!

You are my beloved

You are my heart

You are everything to me

My heart, too, leaps with joy

As it meets yours Spirit to Spirit

(interruption)

What joy you bring to me

You are my loved ones

Live in peace

My peace I leave with you

My beloved

How pleased I am with you

My children, my own

I look at you and I am well pleased

You bring joy to my heart

You have m ear...

Ask for what pleases <u>you</u>

I want to give it to you

Do not hesitate to ask

I want to give you your heart's desire

You fill mine

Come, please your father even more

Let me love you

My Precious Ones

Love me

Love my people

Love me

Act lovingly to my people

Feel my love for them

Know my love for them

Show them that you love them

Through your actions

Through you, then,

They will know that I love them

You know how my loving you feels

Love them so that they

Know how being loved feels

My precious little ones
You are here today to GROW
To grow in the Spirit
To grow in faith
To come closer –
Come closer to me
And to my people
I call you today
To grow in faith
To grow in hope
To grow in love
To grow in charity and good works
In faith – learn and practice your gifts
In hope – let me change you and sharpen your tools
In love – grow to love as I love you
Grow in charity – ah, there is the word to do my work
Practice even those gifts
You may think you do not have
For as you grow in the above
I will increase the tools you have already received
So that you have all you need to minister
To my people – and more –
I will shower you with more than you need
Because those out in the world
Are precious to me too
I love them
Serve them well

(Growth in the Spirit Seminar)

I bless you, my little ones

And press you close to my heart

I love you so, and

What more is there

But to love with all of your being

What more can I say?

But love my people

As I love you

Press them close to your heart

And love them for me

What joy you bring to me

My faithful ones

I see my call to holiness acted upon

Your intercession for those

In pain among you

Your practice of quiet prayer

Lifting up your suffering of your fellow man

And attempting to transcend the pain for others

Yes, you are my own

I claim you

You are mine

CONCLUSION

I suspect that you're reading this after just leafing through the book, without having much of an opportunity to consider the origin of the words or their meaning. I encourage you to take a few minutes to do that now, before continuing -- because.... since there is no commentary in the body of the book within the words, to conclude, I would like to share some of the insights that have come to me in putting the collection together without influencing your thoughts and interpretation. I don't know if you will have a similar response, but this has certainly been a learning experience for me. In one of the words we are told that the Lord likes us to have fun with him, that he likes to play with us (that must be where His joy comes from) - so I thought it might be fun for you to figure out what you think about them... then...look at what I have to say. Seeing the difference in your interpretation and mine will or will not confirm my impressions. Forming your own opinion before you read mine also avoids my coloring your interpretation. It will be interesting to see our differences, and similarities.

I will tell you a story: The Title is:

THE INTERPRETATION

John was a gifted, creative composer who emptied himself into his music. People often said that his symphonies spoke to their hearts, so he understood when they told him of their interpretation of one of his works.

He had just completed a particularly moving symphony, finally choosing a colleague, Al, to conduct the piece and prepare it for the next season's concert series. Al had been his first choice to conduct the piece because they spoke the same language of notes. Al selected Ray, his first chair for the sweet violin solo, because he read between the lines, even though he adhered precisely to his music with few deviances. In the following months of rehearsals each musician in each section considered their interpretation of the piece, with the conductor's focus on the integration and flow.

When it was presented it received a standing ovation. The composer had spoken; the conductor had interpreted and explained; the musicians had interpreted and responded; and the audience had listened, interpreted; and each had received their song.

MY CONCLUSION

Jesus told us that he would not leave us, His Church, orphans - that His Holy Spirit would remain with us (Jn 14) and that He would dwell within us (Jn 14:23). This implies an intimate, personal relationship. How can anyone have an intimate, personal relationship with God? Perhaps an easier question might be - How can you have a relationship with God, much less an intimate relationship? In baby steps perhaps, much like the women in God Calling and Sarah in Jesus Calling.

The question becomes, how are relationships established? More specifically, how are human relationships established? We know how God does it – He reveals himself (Jn 14:21). Revealing oneself means taking a risk – the risk of being vulnerable, of disclosing our innermost selves to one another.

God first revealed Himself when He created a beautiful earth, the waters, the sky, and mankind – It was good. He then revealed exactly who He was in Jesus. He continues to reveal Himself through the Holy Spirit. (Jn 14:21)

In response, how can we let God get to know us? In the same way, by sharing ourselves with Him and others. How can we do that?

People begin to develop a relationship by engaging in mutually shared experiences – they spend time and go places together, develop memories, both happy and sad ("Remember when we....?"), they're engaged in each other's lives, can call them up in the middle of the night if they're lonely, they're able to be themselves and just be present to each other. They must be able to communicate, to have a meaningful exchange, dialogue, as discussed in the Introduction. We are commanded to love one another - how can you love someone you don't know? Have you ever tried to correct someone without an established relationship? How can we be compassionate if not by sharing our most secret selves, our pain? How can we "be there" for others if we can't relate?

Each person in a relationship must feel heard and understood. When one speaks, the other listens, interprets and comprehends (or doesn't). If they haven't heard correctly or don't understand, it must be clarified and said again another way. Then it is the other's turn to speak. When they do "get it" – the relationship comes to life - being heard and understood transforms relationships.

They reveal themselves; they dialogue, they don't monopolize the conversation. The relationship grows in intimacy in relation to the degree that each feel heard. If, in addition, there is a response to what they have said or asked for, the relationship is further strengthened. How better to begin to relate to one another than to listen and respond. We have been invited into a relationship with God the Father, Son and Holy Spirit. The Holy Spirit lingers here among us, waiting to be heard. We can have a relationship with Him, one that is very personal and one that is very intimate. (Jn 14)

TO THE READER

And so, the interpretation of these Words is left to you, the reader. You, their recipient, will now need to discern their origin and value. To me they seem as new and fresh as when I received them.

TO THE CRITIC

I offer these words for public debate, critique, discussion, and to add to the knowledge base. I heard that Robert Frost once said that he couldn't wait for the critics to read his poems so that he could find out what he really meant. That sounds like a good idea for this book too.

I hope that my spirit has met with yours

The collector, not the author

Printed in the United States
By Bookmasters